A LIFE OF
LIBERATION

A Spiritual Guide to Break Free
from Limiting Beliefs and Awakening Your
Potential for Enlightenment

Ryuu Shinohara

A LIFE OF
LIBERATION

The Manifestor Masterlist
(Manifestation has never been
so easy...)

This Masterlist includes:

- Top 3 daily habits for manifesting.
- Simple layout to track your progress.
- Instructions to help you get started today!

The last thing I want is for you to read this book and forget everything you read…

Let's make manifestation a daily habit!

>> Scan the QR Code above with your smartphone to receive your free Manifestor Masterlist. <<

Table of Contents

Introduction

By all factual measures, the world and human civilization is as prosperous as it has ever been. We live longer, healthier lives and our environments do not contain the predators and discomforts that our ancestors had to deal with. Yet, do you feel prosperous? Are you happy?

Worldwide, anxiety and stress levels have continuously risen, despite the progress our societies make. Simply put, a far greater number of people are miserable, and happiness has become a Rubik's Cube to solve. Some seem to have the key to it, but the vast majority don't. If you're reading this book, perhaps you're searching for the solution to this puzzle as well.

So how did we end up here? Where did things go wrong? I mean, happiness is something all of us know innately. When we were children, we had no problem identifying what made us happy and what gave us peace,

but for some reason, as adults, we struggle mightily with this question. Is it the question that is tough to answer or are we simply asking the wrong question?

Your True Problem

The quality of your questions determines the level of insight you will receive. The universe stands ready to grant you everything you need, but this requires you to know which questions to ask in the first place. In fact, most of us have no idea of our own environments and the reality we occupy.

The reason for this distortion is due to our tendency to cling onto our identities. 'I' (the ego) is the most important thing in the world to us. 'Me' (the body) comes in a close second. This illusion of identity is the root cause of a lot of problems since it removes you from acknowledging your place in the greater scheme of things and prevents you from accessing the energy and strength that is on offer for you.

Most of us roam around in this fugue state, not knowing where we are, looking at the wrong things, and thus, is it any wonder that we end up asking all the wrong questions? Even worse, we receive inadequate and

unhelpful answers and end up blaming the scheme that gives us these answers. This is a bit like asking for a lemon and complaining that you had asked for oranges but still receive the lemons!

Only some of us know which questions to ask. Humanity has always had people amongst it who have evolved to a higher plane, Buddha, Jesus, Lao Tzu, and even non-spiritual practitioners. Einstein had written a research paper that allowed us to understand and know that a laser can exist. It was invented 43 years later. The trouble is found in their higher evolutionary thought processes that lead them to speak in a language that few understand. Spiritual advice makes sense and sounds good, but it is unhelpful when it comes to applying it to your own life because you lack the awareness to decipher what is being said.

The disconnection that exists thus frustrates us even more and leads to a vicious circle of search and rejection and then search again when it comes to spiritual solutions to life's problems. Well, this book aims to be the bridge that takes you from your current state of frustration to a state where you can not only ask the right questions but perhaps provide a few answers of your own.

The Nature of Our Reality

A life of liberation is within your sights, and the first step for you to take is to understand the true nature of the reality you occupy. In this book, I will give you all the information you need to learn this. The fact is that this 'ultimate reality' has always been present and still is all around you. It is like your internal organs; you're so accustomed to it that you don't feel it anymore, let alone see it.

The principle of enlightenment and tranquility have been pondered for centuries now. Through the teachings of ancient spiritual instructors and the proof of modern science, it is possible to draw a firm analysis about the world we live in and the nature of our existence. Though, we can only provide you with analysis. To truly understand, you must fall into your own experience. I will show you how these principles can uncover your potential, but until then, I will hold on to the torch and point the way.

The ego is a formidable opponent to your peace and I will show you how to move past it and how you can apply simple spiritual principles to wake up from the illusion. Positive changes in your life are but a step away! All you need to do is walk the path and I will show you exactly how to do this.

Who Am I?

Many years ago, I was in about as bad a place as a teen-ager could be. My mind was wracked by thoughts of inadequacy and anxiety. I meant to do well but for some reason, the results would never come and I would end up making things more complicated for myself. It seemed as if everyone else knew something I didn't.

This led to a massive loss of self-esteem and feelings of guilt caused by the thoughts of letting the people around me down constantly. Was this the true reason for my exis-tence? Well, it certainly seemed true to me. What is truth anyway? Is it what seems real to us and our experience or is it some objective thought based on past conditioning? This got me thinking and I realized that there were large gaps in my knowledge.

Thus began my study of philosophers and spiritual guides which lasted for a decade and still continues. Alan Watts, Vadim Zeland, Terrance Mckenna, and the likes of many more became my constant companions. To say that I was obsessed is to miss the point of my learning. After all, I could see how my life was involving all these factors, and I felt that I owed it to myself and to some-thing greater than me to pursue knowledge in these areas.

It wasn't long before I realized that my true happiness lies in my everyday experience. I look for God, Toa, Brahman, (or whatever you wish to call IT) in everything and everyone. To see the infamous 'I Am' in others, to see textures becoming animated and vivid, to see the underlying gleam in the eyes and actions of the modern man as one sees when holding a baby or a puppy.

I will point your worldview in this direction, so you can see what I am referring to. I can only play with the words. You must express yourself the way you see fit. My philosophy and the information I have presented in this book are founded on the basic principles of nature that have been established for millennia now.

The keys to your liberation are not hidden; they are actually extremely obvious. Following these basic principles will help you realize the inner tension that creates negativity and seems to follow you wherever you go. You will uncover the happiness that has been hidden from you since your early childhood.

When you align yourself to your true nature, your ability to influence the external world and create exactly what you want accelerates, and you need not live the same old life of being trapped by circumstances outside (as well as inside) of you. Don't judge yourself harshly for

living like this. You've been influencing and manifesting everything, but you just don't realize it yet!

You see, you aren't blind at all. You've just been walking around with your eyes closed, thinking you're blind. By directing your thoughts and allowing them to flow, you will be able to set the course and will know exactly what to do. We lose a sense of our course when we completely stay fixated on the boat rather than the sun and stars.

Eckhart Tolle did 'nothing' for two years and lived on a park bench completely transfixed. Eventually, he found his calling and became a spiritual teacher. What is your true calling? How do you currently see the world? Are you seeing what is true? I will help you open your eyes and experience the positive changes that the people who sought my help have experienced.

My Promise

The knowledge of how to bridge the gap between your current life and the life you are meant to live has been passed down for centuries. I will help you attend to this knowledge for you to build your own bridge. It is up to you to walk the path that will take you to the other side and realize the promised land for yourself.

Along the way, I will be there by your side, constantly guiding you and helping you forward. The key is to acknowledge and experience the beauty of where you are now. Once a person has experienced this, there is no going back and you will find the fruits of your dreams waiting for you.

To realize all this though, you need to allow your sense of being to mature. Give up control of the process and instead allow your awareness to grow and cultivate a life of its own. Much like the blooming of a flower, the event cannot be forced. It can only be nurtured and taken care of. When you nurture the awareness of an experience with unforced gratitude, positive intentions, and unconditional love, you will have no other place to be but here and now.

The Time Is Now

Our world is changing at a pace hitherto unknown. The pace of this change has caught everybody off guard and the inability to cope with these changes has led to misery and suffering around the world. Humanity is particularly ripe for this liberation. To become adaptable in an exponentially growing world is much needed.

Stop experiencing the effects of negativity that is born from your lack of understanding. Stop the unnecessary mental suffering, both your own and the suffering that you unwittingly create for those around you. Free yourself from your illusion and suffering and live the life you were meant to live right now.

This guide is your trusted companion as you walk the path of liberation. Also known as the "direct path" in Buddhism. Anxiety, depression, sadness, and so on will evaporate once you realize the wisdom presented here.

So stop feeding negativity in your life and stop your suffering. Begin your journey and create your experiences starting now!

CHAPTER 1

The Origins of Spiritual Liberation

Human beings have always pondered the nature of human existence. As unbelievable as it might sound, the problems that the ancient civilizations faced and the ones that you face, spiritually speaking, are the same. The ancients figured out philosophy, expressed as religion, and found a path to their liberation.

In the west, we tend to separate philosophical from religious thought, with the nature of God and Man existing as dual couples. This leads to confusion when studying eastern scriptures since there is no duality in these teachings. So who is correct? What is the truth?

Well, in this chapter I hope to lift the veil from these seemingly diverse schools of thought and show you that in the end, all is one of the same.

Eastern and Western Philosophy

The first question we have to ask ourselves here is whether the distinction between eastern and western thought is useful in the first place? After all, drawing a geographical line between the two seems a bit arbitrary. However, there is no denying that when beginning to study both schools of thought, it certainly helps to draw such a distinction.

For one, western philosophy, as practiced by the ancient Greeks and Romans, places a huge burden on empiricism and the necessity of applying the scientific process to natural observations. The primary concern for these institutions are to deal with such questions as "What is the meaning of all this?" or "What is beyond death?", there isn't much mention of divinity or of liberation in terms of rationalized theory.

Eastern thought is more holistic, in the sense that there is no distinction between this world and the one above or below it (or as they say in the east 'behind it') Everyone is merely playing in a whole picture that none of us can escape from. In order to better understand the

similarities between both sides, it is well worth exploring their differences.

While modern western philosophy does not consume the religious angle, this was not always the case. The foundation of all western philosophy was established by the ancient Greeks who were deeply concerned with the idea of 'Eudaimonia' (good life). This deep concern led to the establishment of a number of schools of thought, with the most famous being the Sophists, considered the school of Socrates and Stoicism, whose principles exist to this day.

Seneca, one of the most popular philosophers from the Stoic school of thought, encapsulated the idea behind this philosophy when he admonished his friends' complaints when things didn't work out for them. Since all of life was constant suffering, what was the point of mourning a solitary event?

Stoic philosophy is not meant to be pessimistic and is often misunderstood. The point Seneca was trying to make was that an equanimous mind is the key to dealing with the way the chaotic world works. It is not the result of events that upset us but our expectations. When we create expectations for something and it doesn't go according to our script, our dissatisfaction compounds

and creates a psychological smoothie called misery and depression, all thanks to our hopes being dashed and restimulated by memory.

The solution to this is to not have any expectations in the first place and maintain a slightly balanced and almost pessimistic view of things. By doing so, if things work out, we receive a pleasantly surprising jolt of happiness, and if they don't, we're no worse off than before. This reducing of excessive emotional attachment or importance to the outcome keeps the mind's balance maintained. The key is to avoid the extremes and not float around like a lifeless body that doesn't care about anything or anybody.

The writings of Marcus Aurelius flow in the same direction, and he is considered one of the most prominent Stoic philosophers. The large majority of ancient western philosophy is concerned with human beings accepting their place in nature. In this regard, there isn't a lot of difference with eastern thought.

Answers to questions such as "how to best live life" and the true meaning of things such as virtue and ethics dominate the conversation. A key characteristic of all schools of philosophical thought is that they prescribe action. Every school, be it Epicurean, Stoic or Sophist, prescribes certain actions that ought to be carried out in order to attain the state of virtue, which is the ideal state of happiness, or it's key.

The eastern schools take a different approach to this. Using the example of ancient Hinduism and Buddhism, it is not action that is prescribed but rather, a curious form of inaction that the Chinese call Wu-Wei or 'not doing'. These schools of thought ascribe a lot of power to the nature in Man, which is the whole universe, and being hypnotized to appear as mere egos creates the human being's ultimate aim; the ultimate realization or remembrance of 'I Am'. This realization is often referred to as the state of Nirvana.

If all the prescriptions needed to be reduced to a single idea, it is to accept and allow. The best way to live a good life, according to eastern philosophy, is to accept and allow the present moment to unfold as it will, yet this doesn't imply that you let yourself be taken advantage of. Feel free to make all the plans you want, but understand that your plans are a lot like drawing on water. Ultimately, you need to go in whichever direction the water takes you and it is foolish to resist, like swimming against the current.

"No valid plans for the future can be made by those who have no capacity for living now"- Alan Watts

Thus, the actions that need to be taken involve dissolving the false attachments we have to our egos, which (by western thought) is considered imperfect. What is perfection then? Well, the state of your current being is of itself perfect and only when a person realizes this can their so-called 'binds' evaporate. All that you are, your ego, your thoughts, your emotions, are in the foreground of being, which is a perfect process that keeps the world animated and alive. Otherwise, without the ego, we would be working to sustain our neighbor's rent, buy them food, chew their food, and if at all possible digest it for them.

As you can see, while ancient western thought was primarily concerned with trying to control the aspects of life that could be controlled and often ended up taking a pessimistic view of things, eastern thought ascribed divinity to things that could not be controlled and sought to explain the cause of suffering by attributing a higher knowledge to it. You don't need to know why something is happening apart from that it is good for you.

By contrast, western thought can be summarized as saying 'don't worry about what is happening, this is merely another misfortune in a greater tragedy'. They might be talking about the same thing but the approach is completely different. Eventually, both civilizations descended into chaos and ignorance, with the west plunged into the dark ages and the east stuck in darkness for the most part to this day.

The Renaissance saved the west from going the way of the east thanks to the birth of the scientific process and for the first time in centuries, dogma was openly questioned once again. The most fascinating development out of all of this was that the majority of scientists considered themselves philosophers because for the first time in human history, truth could be discovered via rationality.

Thus, the prevailing religious undertones that philosophy had acquired at the time began to shed. We'll look at religious thought in the next section. Anyway, this uncoupling of philosophical from religious thought led to the devaluation of nature as a wise force. After all, nature was viewed as chaos and thanks to the scientific process prescribing rationality above all else, man was viewed as the master of everything. This established a somewhat adversarial relationship with nature.

17

Key elements from ancient philosophy remained. The idea that man's true nature ultimately didn't add up to much and that when designing systems of government, it was best to design it to withstand attack and error, as opposed to designing something that was the most rational. Western thought did skirt onto eastern ground occasionally, notably with Baruch Spinoza's ideas of considering everything 'under the aspect of eternity'.

As the western powers expanded their political reach, thanks to the fruits of the scientific process, they came into touch with eastern thought via colonialism. While it was easy to dismiss eastern philosophy as pagan nonsense at first, as science began to advance, it was hard to ignore the fact that scientific conclusions were often in agreement with what ancient eastern philosophy stated.

A prime example of this is the Buddha's assertion that everything in this world exists in impermanence. Every object in this world vibrates and that the things that appear solid are actually just vibrating at a lower frequency. The quantum theory and quantum mechanics, fields discovered by Neils Bohr, describe this situation perfectly.

Thus began a process of the movement of western thought towards eastern principles and the recognition

of the role of emotion as an equal of rationality. While rationality is a process one attaches to the brain, emotions are something that emanates from the heart. Reality now began to be seen as a combination of both forces, instead of advocating the advantage of one over the other.

I'll discuss this more in the section dealing with the similarities and connections. For now, let us fill the gaping hole in our narrative that has been caused by my skipping over the religious doctrine of Christianity.

Christianity

With the decline of the Western Roman Empire came the rise of Christianity and it duly filled the gap that was caused both politically as well as philosophically. Of course, Christianity being a religion, caused people to become occupied by a merciless God who sought to rid the world of its sins.

Non-pagan religions placed a huge emphasis on the prospect of salvation and while the term is quite similar to Liberation (in Hindu Moksha), the spirit of it is quite different. While the eastern pagan religions saw everything as being one with the flow of nature, the newer religions (Christianity and Islam), envisioned a world where

the pessimistic bent of western philosophy was taken to its extreme.

In this world view, heaven existed as a place above Earth, while hell existed as the place below it. While ancient Greek religion depicted the world similarly, it didn't quite carry over into philosophy as much as it did at this time in the world's history. Salvation became a process of following God's word to the T and ignoring a lot of human tendencies and sacrificing them at the altar of God.

Christian philosophy and the religious prescriptions contained within can be seen as extreme exaggerations of previous philosophical thought. We've already seen how the Stoic concept of suffering became 'sin' versus 'salvation'. In addition to this, human beings often resorted to their worst instincts, which became the infallibility of God and the complete ignorance of man.

While a lot of Christian principles are born from political and power struggles, there's no denying that the moral code that was applied had its origins in conventional thought. Thus, there are many similarities with eastern thought, but their interpretations are being diametrically opposed to one another.

As an example, ancient Hindu scriptures contain numerous stories of the fallibility of the Gods, they look

upon the world as a play, an act of pure drama, where at the end of the play the masks are removed. Zen Buddhism sees the world as an organism, organic, and self-structuring. And so gives rise as a philosophy filled with contradicting ideas, often played with by Monks to enlighten their disciples.

However, to merely read Buddhist scripture does not explain Zen. No amount of books can explain Zen. Practice is often the solution to the discomfort but when we view Zen as the ultimate truth, it transforms from a practice or way of living in the world to an idea, dogma, or system of empowerment that allows our reasoning mind to be comforted.

Taoism is in the same boat, they see nature as a self occurring and harmonious event that should be translated within human action and thought, and the entire philosophy is geared towards realizing this truth.

Contrast this with the almighty smiter who appears in the Old Testament and we can safely conclude that although the ideas of these religions have a common seed, their ways of expressing them are diametrically opposite.

I do not present this information with the intention of showing you which one is superior or which one works better. My point is that no matter the source of your

beliefs, understanding the truth involves you studying the similarities at their roots. Often, we take the differences to heart and believe that a certain philosophy provides a better prescription.

This is a man-made construct and obscures the truth. In other words, every religion and philosophy has constructs within it that result from the ego and not form a perfect understanding of the way the world works. In order to recognize the truth, you need to see the world for what it is, beyond or 'behind' these constructs and reason lies an undefinable reality.

All is One

In order to fully process religious and philosophical doctrine, it is important to grind them down to certain basic truths. Ultimately, what is the point of all of this? On the surface of it, Zen Buddhism and the writings of Immanuel Kant don't have much in common. However, by reducing or following everything down to their base concepts, we begin to see the truth in everything.

Think of it this way. Different forms of music exist, from rock to rap to classical to jazz. A rock ballad is not going to sound anything like a baroque classical orchestra. Yet, both forms of music evoke something deeply

fundamental in us. They evoke a certain truth, and this truth is experienced as a feeling that cannot be described rationally.

When speaking of music, we can think of this feeling as bliss or excitement or whatever you want to call it. When speaking of religion and philosophy though, what feelings do they evoke? What is the purpose of it all? In a word: Salvation.

Salvation, meaning to save, is something that deeply moves us. Whether it is rescuing ourselves from bad situations or preventing someone else from making a mistake, ultimately our goal in life is to be liberated from it all. In the Christian sense, salvation is seen as a persons' body-mind ascending from this world to the heavenly one above. Salvation in Christianity isn't easy in the eyes of the Christian. You're judged at the pearly gates and only the worthy may enter. Similar sentiments prevail in Islam.

In Hinduism and Taoism, salvation (liberation) can be thought of as the realization of Moksha, even if the latter doesn't use that particular term. Traditional Buddhism, practiced in the Indian subcontinent, evokes similar terms to describe the realization of enlightenment.

Zen, Tibetan, and Chinese Buddhist principles describe similar outcomes as well.

Ultimately, salvation, liberation, awakening, freedom, all of them are the common goal of everything we have discussed thus far. This is the common ground on which everything and everyone agrees. How well do we understand it though?

Salvation as a Philosophy

The Christian method of salvation is to focus on the avoidance of sin. This is in keeping with the pessimistic approach of the monotheistic religions which paints salvation or attaining the abode of God as an extremely difficult task and one that is beyond the reach of most men.

With the default mode of man being one of sins, the necessity for a savior arises and this is what Jesus is. Through Jesus (or Mohammed) God's wishes for man are communicated and the best way to serve God is to 'worship' his wishes and live in accordance to them. While this seems a harsh method of attaining salvation, there is no denying that the intention here is one that benefits our lives.

Such an interpretation doesn't leave a lot of room for spirituality. With it being reduced to simple God and

man dynamic, the average person doesn't have too much room to explore what is within them, seeing as salvation is reduced to, largely, following rules. (I'm aware that I'm simplifying a lot here.)

Eastern religion provides a lot more room for spiritual liberation by exploring the nature of God itself. Vedanta philosophy provides perhaps the most easily understood interpretation of them all. The main construct of this world, the Self if you will, is termed Brahman, and everything that exists in this world is but a part of Brahman. Similar statements can be found in Christianity as well which mentions that everything is created in the image of God.

Vedanta differs from Christianity in that it then proceeds to say that the realization of Brahman (the Christian God), is found within oneself since man is but a part of Brahman and has no individual self of his or her own. Therefore, salvation lies in looking within and respecting the wishes of your heart since this is your connection to Brahman.

Religions all over mention the connection of your heart to whichever brand of God they espouse, so everyone is in agreement here. Even the inherent concept of Vedanta, the singular Brahman, is given expression in

various ways, as Allah, God, The Ineffable etc. by all religions. It is at this point that the ego interferes and sullies things.

The creation of differences is a result of the ego driving thoughts and desperately needing to carve an identity for itself. This is what results in Islamic and Christian doctrines appearing opposite to one another when the truth is that everything talks about the same thing. Our innate knowing of nonduality is truth, whereas the ego is obsessed with duality and takes on a life of its own at the forefront of our experience.

Dual and Nondual

Once you begin to recognize the truth of nonduality, everything begins to simplify itself. There is no you versus the world. You are the world. There is no God separate from you. God is you and around you since everything is one. Even the ego is one with God, it just needs and craves an identity out of individuation, which is not to be confused with separation.

This is how cultural differences manifest as warring nations and religious philosophy becomes a referendum on the state of the world. The ego needs emotional drama, and most of all, it needs time. It is no different of the idea of liberation needing a sense of self-abidance.

The ego creates mental hierarchies and rules in order to attain this, but the reality is that all of it is a false illusion.

The ego convinces you that living life a certain way is the way to walk the path to liberation when the truth is that liberation or God is already present in everything. If God is present in everything, the path of the fool or the path of the criminal is as equally spiritual as that of the saint or sage. This is a huge blow to the ego since by putting it on a par with the dregs of society, we damage its need for an identity and its need to develop a favorable comparison to satisfy itself.

The true spiritual path to liberation lies in merely recognizing that everything has a right to exist, even negativity, since existence is in the background of everything (physical or metaphysical) you could say that existence is God and through God is where you find liberation, that is, through existing in your everyday experience. Realize the connection you have to the universe, but do not hang onto it, for if you do, you will only strangle it. Life is a living and fragile 'thing' to be reconciled, not choked and strangled to death for drops of happiness and love. The only way to retrieve happiness is to let go of it, a way that Alan Watts termed "The Law of Reversed Effort". The universe works in much the same manner.

"For whoever desires to save his life will lose it, and who-ever will lose his life will find it." -Matthew 16:25

Desire is an egotistical construct that convinces us that the attainment of something external or internal will fulfill our lives. Whether it is a certain body, a new car, or a mental state, they are all objective and have no true ground to who we are. Paradoxically, it is perfectly possible to desire a state of non-desiring, and this is the vicious circle the large majority of people in the world find themselves in. By practicing rituals and chanting hymns, all we're doing is giving voice to our ego's desire to feel good about itself.

The ego is an image of our separate selves and not of our individual selves; its highest meaning lies in duality and separation. If true reality is nondual, it follows that the ego is a false construct, it doesn't exist (subjectively). This mirage disappears the closer you get to it; in other words, there is no 'person' or 'ego' to find. The 'ego' from now till the end of this book will mean "the mirage of separateness".

But also notice, the things that I mentioned that the ego creates are not inherently bad. It is our lack of awareness that twists it into negativity and manifests

this in our lives. The way forward then is to realize non-duality and to simply continue living. How does one make sense of this? How is it true when it is not in our current experience?

Letting Go

Much like how exhaling is crucial to regaining your breath, you need to let go of your need for liberation in order to realize it. In reality, there is no 'part' where you 'attain' a certain state of consciousness that is different from the previous one. You need to recognize that liberation lies in the here and now, that is to say in heaven and in hell. For you to be able to recognize your connection to nondual experience, you must genuinely realize this truth.

Liberation ultimately implies freedom, and most people take this to mean that they are free to do as they please. Does this mean if you so desire, you could get rid of depression and anxiety as you please? For all these mental states are caused by our thinking; in other words, do you choose your own thoughts? Try to think of your ideal paradise for the whole day without a single other thought jumping in. Can you? Our mental unease is not caused by uncontrolled thinking; it is caused by our

lack of uncontrolled thinking. Anxiety and depression arise when we resist and damn up these random and fluid thoughts by attempting to take control of them. In other words, you are not free until you are free to think as you please.

If you so choose to experience liberation and bliss, you must realize that in order to do so, should you not be free and liberated to do the things that you do not want in equal measure. Just as God created the world of opposites, you too are living in a world that must balance between the negative as much as the positive. Consciousness requires this incorporation of negative feedback, as Dr. Maxwell Maltz proved in his book Psycho Cybernetics. You cannot realize breathing unless you let it go and you can only recognize the value of freedom by letting go of your need for it. This is the same conclusion that can be found in Tao philosophy with the description of Yin and Yang energies.

Note that I don't mean to say you should not want liberation. It is when you begin to desire it that you stop allowing it to grow in the background. To desire something is to strangle it, so let yourself breathe, let go of yourself, grow, and take shape. Allow IT to exist. Allow

yourself to exist. The freedom to allow yourself to do things you don't want is merely allowing yourself to exist as you are.

If you recognize yourself as a reflection of God, you will realize that you need not worry about experiencing some stated ideal for the sake of liberation. You simply need to live. You can be stupid, you can be morose, you can be miserable. Ultimately, God resides within you, and your realization of God will take place despite the seeming negativity within you.

Realizing God or spiritual enlightenment is not about building yourself up to something. It is simply recognizing that behind this person called 'Susan' lies an infinite sea of awareness that peeks through the windows of your sense perceptions. Enlightenment lies in the movement of the present and not the destination. Thus, going back to our previous question of whether you should choose your thoughts and rid of depression and anxiety, liberation lies in realizing that all this mental "stuff" is a process that must be accepted, like the process of precipitation. For when it rains we feel cold, we hide away and wait for the sun. But the secret lies in dancing or playing in the rain, much like a child does.

"Some people feel the rain. Others just get wet."
-Bob Marley

Liberation then lies in maintaining a state of equanimity where you are perfectly free to want something but recognize that the act of wanting has no power to control you or warp your mind.

You are free to want it and are free from wanting it at the same time. There is no duality. You are equally free to not want it as well since achieving it isn't linked to your identity in any way, which is what your ego convinces you. There is no time by which you 'have to' experience something since time is a construct of the ego mirage; time does not exist in the same space as experience.

God and Liberation is not about where you want to be or who you want to become. It is right where you are and how you live right now.

CHAPTER 2

A Spiritual Connection With The Brain: Understanding the Science

Science and spirituality have begun interacting with one another in far greater frequency recently. Part of this is simply the world's need to make sense of the multitude of changes we are going through, which is unprecedented at any point in human history. Another reason for this interaction is that as technology gets better, a lot of scientific research drills down to basic causes, and there emerges a natural connection.

Ultimately, there isn't a lot of divergence between spirituality and science. The disconnect that currently

exists is only because of technological limitations that prevent science from exploring things further. However, the things we know are powerful enough to take a deeper look at.

Thought Patterns and Beliefs

A popular concept in spirituality right now is 'flow'. The flow state refers to a state of mind where you are completely absorbed in the present, your actions are automatically fluid and performance levels shoot through the roof. You essentially feel your best and perform your best. Jamie Weil characterizes it as S.T.E.R

S) Selflessness. Your sense of self (ego) completely vanishes. It is a feeling of losing yourself and discovering Self. It is the experience of pure psychological liberation.

T) Timelessness. The way the brain manages time gets shut down. It no longer feels trapped and bonded. Time passes unorthodoxly fast or slow.

E) Effortlessness. You feel as though there are no strains or restrictions in your actions or thoughts. Every move perfectly followed by the next.

R) Richness. A sense of information overload. You process and access more information quickly. You're no longer thinking linearly, you recognize patterns easily, and there is a higher chance of taking risks.

All of these characters light up at the same time; it is the ultimate human state of consciousness that cannot be fully translated. Much like channeling or how an artist paints or a musician creates work that they don't really know where it's coming from, achieving a flow state has become a goal of sorts for a lot of new-age spiritual gurus.

A flow state is often thought of as a primarily spiritual concept and is something that is experienced when we surrender ourselves to something greater. What I mean is that achieving a flow state requires us to recognize that there is a presence that resides within us, which has access to the intelligence of Mother Nature. I.e. infinite intelligence. IT flows through us and knows the result of every possible permutation and combination that will result from our actions.

This concept is often found in religion. We've just seen in the previous chapter how Vedanta philosophy talks about the presence of Brahman, which is the source of everything. Catholicism talks of God in the same manner, and every spiritual practice refers to this all-knowing power.

How does one 'let go' and give in to this power? Well, a lot of it has to do with risk-taking and getting out of your own way. We tend to develop mental structures that

hinder us when we're under pressure, and this warps our view of things. All of us have experience with this happening. When we're fully relaxed and unhurried, we tend to see things differently than when we're tense.

Anxiety and depression, or any form of stress really, warp our minds. Research conducted by neuroscientists supports this view. In a famous study carried out on the Israeli defense forces, two images were shown to them, with the first containing a blurred image of Saturn and the second containing just a fuzzy image of nothing in particular.

When relaxed, the troops were able to correctly spot that there was no pattern to the fuzz in the second image while there was an image of Saturn in the first beneath the fuzz. However, when asked prior to a parachute jump, the troops began seeing a pattern in the second image.

This is a pretty good illustration of how anxiety warps our minds, and this is the exact opposite of the flow state of mind. Stress and anxiety can be thought of as applying the brakes to the natural acceleration force that your brain possesses. Your brain is a natural problem-solving machine and is always seeking to find the best solutions to what lies ahead of it.

However, we tend to apply the brakes using beliefs and constructs that emanate from our self-image. Put it this way: Your brain is perfectly capable of helping you realize the life that you want to live. However, if you don't believe this is possible, you throw a barrier in its way and pump the brakes on whatever momentum the brain naturally tries to create.

Our self-image is something that is learned at a very young age when we're completely helpless. As children, we surrender completely to our environment and to those around us because we realize deep down that our chances of survival without them is pretty low. There is a certain freedom in this surrender because it lifts worries from our shoulders. We can sleep peacefully, knowing that someone else will take care of our problems.

It shouldn't come as a surprise then, that this pattern of thinking follows us into adulthood. As adults, we're responsible for fixing everything that is wrong in our lives, and this is a significant source of stress for us. Since achieving the flow state of being, where things solve themselves (seemingly) requires us to get rid of stress, the solution is to adopt the same tactics we employed as children.

In other words, surrender to your own actions. The force you surrender to this time is not your parents or

guardians but the intelligence of nature. The same intelligence that beats your heart and digests your food. Science cannot fully explain this via research, but there is no denying the sense of relief that accompanies us when we realize that all of our problems are being taken care of and that we need not worry about them with the same intensity.

There is still the issue with our self-image pressing the brakes on our ambitions. Why does our own brain hinder us in this manner? After all, if it is designed to solve problems, surely it makes no sense that the brain will stop itself? Well, the answer is revealed when we view our self-image as a survival mechanism.

As much as the brain is inclined to solve problems, its greatest function is to help you survive. This is where your ego and belief system enter the picture and work in tandem with your automatic brain, which is the part of your brain that doesn't require conscious thought to activate itself, to keep you safe. When you walk into a forest and see a bear running towards you, you know exactly what to do.

The modern world is not a very good place for this automatic mechanism since we live in largely sterile environments. The biggest danger to us is our fellow man and

not something nature cooked up. Thus, our perception of what is dangerous is significantly warped. The place that a bear occupies is now shared with not being able to land a lucrative job offer and so on.

The survival mechanism naturally puts our bodies under stress since in real life or death situations we need that additional boost to save ourselves. A byproduct of this is stress. With the modern world having warped our minds to the extent that we cannot recognize truly life-threatening situations, our survival instinct is always on and stress is omnipresent.

Surrender is therefore a powerful mechanism to combat this. Relaxing into the knowledge that you don't know everything and that this is perfectly fine since there is someone bigger than you taking care of things, is perhaps the ultimate relaxation mechanism. Meditation is one method of practicing this.

Research has shown that meditation, defined as the practice of being aware of oneself dispassionately, tends to slow down the areas of the brain that pumps the brakes on the automatic creative mechanism inside our brains. The automatic creative mechanism is simply the result of evolution and the way our species has adapted to survive.

Spiritual ideas of the existence of a benevolent greater power aiding us make more sense when viewed through the prism of evolution. While everyone usually thinks of the principle of survival of the fittest when talking of evolution, the truth is that Darwin's ideas extend far beyond this small topic. The survival of the fittest principle is misunderstood in that it is thought of as nature weeding out the unworthy when really, the process of adaptation is just nature providing everything within it the tools to evolve and survive better.

We see examples of this all around us. People who refuse to change are doing so voluntarily. There is nothing in nature that forces us to remain the same and it takes a lot of effort to remain in one place for a long time. When viewed like this, you can understand my point about the survival of the fittest being a benevolent principle and not one that is based on culling the unworthy.

The flow state is simply the result of evolution and is nature's way of helping us develop solutions to our problems. Throwing up barriers to it is simply the ego exerting itself by saying, 'this is who I am'. We've already seen in the previous chapter why the idea of 'you' is a false construct. Resting into your existence and surrendering to a greater power is the easiest method of achieving this flow state.

You may ask, is there a greater power scientifically speaking? My response is, who cares? Science cannot prove, currently, the existence of a greater power without a shadow of a doubt. However, neuroscientists do agree on the power of surrender as a tool to fight our negative beliefs. So why not use it to your advantage?

Brain Waves

Your brain is a collection of neurons and neural networks. Neurons are what brain cells are called, and a collection of brain cells that are joined together form a neural network. The interesting thing about neurons is that their activity is almost entirely electrical in nature. When a particular belief or thought is activated, it is really just an electrical network comprised of neurons that are firing together.

By its very nature, electricity produces electromagnetic waves, and the environment within our brain is no exception. Scientists can measure the frequency of these waves and can accurately determine what sort of a state our brain is currently in. Brain waves are a revolutionary concept because not only can you use them to figure out what is going on inside your head but also use them to stimulate certain states of mind in order to experience liberation.

First, let's take a quick look at the different types of brain waves that exist.

Delta Waves

Delta waves are the slowest in frequency and usually occur during deep sleep. These waves are found to exist for longer periods in infants and children as opposed to adults. Given that they occur during deep sleep, you can guess that these waves are associated with deep relaxation and regenerative healing.

Deep states of fully detached meditation also produce delta waves, although meditation produces different waves as well.

Theta Waves

Up one level in terms of frequency are theta waves. These waves also occur during sleep and are associated with healing and relaxation. In addition to this, research shows that theta waves occur when our brains are in the process of embedding memories or in dreaming states. The other state, when theta waves occur, are states between sleep and wakefulness, in other words, before full consciousness.

In a theta state, we can experience unconscious memories as well as intense emotions. Anyone who has ever woken up feeling extreme emotions can attest to this fact. Theta waves are useful for learning and memory consolidation.

Alpha Waves

Alpha waves occur at the lowest frequency during our wakeful state. This frequency usually results in us being relaxed and contemplating something deeply. The connection between our minds and bodies is highest during this time, and we have full access to our creative and intellectual faculties.

People who spend a lot of time contemplating things or learn things well are usually vibrating in an alpha state of mind. Despite being awake, this is a state of relaxation where a lot of ideas come together, and insights can be gained.

Beta Waves

This is the most common state of mind we exist in. Beta waves occur during most periods of conscious thought and are present during social interactions, problem-solv-

ing, and other tasks that require focus. Beta waves can be thought of like a double-edged sword since they assist us in solving problems, but an excess of them can lead to problems like stress and anxiety.

When our brain is busy deciphering patterns, beta waves are generated. As you can imagine, without adequate levels of relaxation, we begin to see things that don't exist, and this causes even more problems.

Gamma Waves

These waves have the highest levels of frequency and don't occur very often. During these states, scientists have observed that every part of the brain is accessible and is working to solve the problem together. The flow of information is rapid, and there are no barriers whatsoever.

Physically, we experience this state as a flash of insight or in the form of developing a creative solution to a problem we've been wrestling with for a while. Interestingly, research shows that Tibetan monks who are well versed in their meditation practice can seemingly produce these waves at will and for longer periods of.

The reason for this is that a state of love or loving-kindness produces gamma waves within us. Again, we see evidence of how spirituality and science speak the

same language, even if the words are different. The state of loving-kindness is thought of as being connected to everything around us and of being in the flow state.

This interconnectedness is proved by science by the fact that our brain is fully accessible during this state. It is easy to make the connection between this fact and the spiritual assertion that God or knowledge resides within us. Scientific proof does not exist to explain how or why a jump occurs from a theta state to a gamma state during meditation. Spirituality tells us this is simply the realization of God, but that doesn't provide much scientific fact. For now, we do know that it exists, but the exact process, biologically speaking, is not known.

Yoga and meditation help awaken ideal states of the mind within us. Do not make the mistake of thinking that one type of brain wave is better than the other. The truth is that everyone needs a different cocktail of brain waves to help them get past their own challenges. The exact combination needs to be felt, rather than thought of logically.

Our minds will communicate to us what it needs most in the moment, so staying in the present is a valuable tool in all of this. Perhaps this is why meditation aids the process of developing ideal states of mind to the extent that

it does. While the gamma states of mind are desirable, this state is not something that can be grasped at.

Gamma states of mind usually result from allowing them to enter, much like we saw in the previous chapter. Meditation and yoga can be thought of as the practice of allowing consciousness to express itself through mind and body awareness. This state of being might mean you vibrate at an alpha level, sometimes at the beta level, and so on. Every vibration has a certain purpose, and discounting one in favor of another is the wrong approach.

However, this doesn't mean you need to adopt a completely passive approach to the way your brain waves exist within you. You can consciously try to increase your level of creativity or your ability to process information with deep insight. As I've already mentioned, yoga and meditation create certain states of mind that can also help improve your awareness of the moment.

Other ways of improving your mental state include changing your environment. Our environment has a huge impact on us even to this day. When we are children, the majority of our beliefs are created thanks to the environment we are exposed to. It stands to reason then, that if you wish to develop certain states of being within you, changing your environment helps immensely.

For example, if your wish is to develop a greater sense of insight, associate with people who spend their time thinking and exercising their brains with deep thought. Sages have a presence that permeates our mind and body, and as it stands, have a great part in an individual's path to liberation. You do not need to meet these people physically. The beauty of the internet is that information is available everywhere, and it is possible to associate with people by listening to their ideas and exposing yourself to this information.

Books remain an evergreen source of self-improvement and anyone who is remotely intelligent reads. These days, audiobooks provide a wonderful way to consume knowledge if reading isn't exactly your thing. Another way to improve your overall state of being is to take supplements or nootropics. I won't go into too much detail but, scientists are now referring the gut as our second brain. Probiotics, prebiotics, and multivitamins are known to alleviate brain fog, anxiety, depression, and overall mood. Consuming high quality, chemical-free whole foods has often been advocated as the best diet as well, and there is a lot of wisdom in this.

Food doesn't affect your brainwaves specifically as much as it affects your overall brain connections. Most

importantly, it helps promote healthy digestion and gut health. There is increasing research that shows that our gut health is linked to our state of mind and that states of anxiety and depression often originate from the gut.

Lastly, you can use brainwave entrainment technology. I must mention that these brainwave techniques and practices are to help you experience different states of consciousness and can help you feel more relaxed and calm. Liberation does not include any form of "trying". We are more interested in carving a path of least resistance for your mind and body to sink deeper into awareness and realization. Either way, there is no denying that these methods help you focus on your tasks better and produce higher quality work.

CHAPTER 3

The False Self - Ego

As you journey along your path to spiritual liberation, you will encounter your false and separate self, also called your ego. The ego would truly be a marvel of creation if it weren't so bad for us. The ego has many different constructs and works in ways that will amaze you to learn.

Accepting the ego, as opposed to destroying it, is crucial for the realization of peace in your life. To understand the process of acceptance, it is necessary to understand the nature of the ego and the things that drive it. As I said before, "This mirage disappears the closer you get to it..."

Identification with Our Thoughts

The creation of the ego has its roots in the creation of our identity. A self-image, a definition of 'who I am' is

an essential aspect of existence because this plays a vital role in helping us get in touch with our true nature and the purpose of our existence. Your self-image is some combination of who you are meant to be, as per divine design, along with the impact your environment makes upon you.

If we recognize and stay close to the true nature of our existence, it is pretty much impossible for the ego to develop. However, the ego is essential for our initial detachment coming into this world. Other than that, it is almost completely useless. It finds fertile ground to grow thanks to the way our societies approach the topics of education and self-development.

A certain amount of material possessions is required in order to live a fulfilling life. Walking in the cold without the protection of a coat or in the rain without an umbrella will consign us to a pretty miserable existence indeed. The mistake lies in attaching meaning to these material objects as being the purpose for living and forgetting that all they do is perform a function.

Soon, we begin to attach these material objects (including our bodies) to our identities, and this is where the ego springs into action and reinforces these ideas. Thus, what began as a good idea turns into something else entirely.

The ego is difficult to root out precisely because of this. It springs from good intentions and cloaks itself with the protection that these intentions provide, scaring us into thinking that the destruction of the ego will lead to the destruction of these intentions and consign us to a miserable life.

Nothing could be farther from the truth.

Ego Identification

Ego identification refers to mental constructs that cause us to mistake the ego as being our true identity. When this happens, the ego begins to function as a living organism and demands the protection and survival mechanisms that all living organisms need. This is an absurd state of affairs because the ego is simply a thought pattern.

It is not physical by any means and hence cannot be hurt by outside circumstances. If negative occurrences like hunger or thirst were to strike, they strike the physical body. The ego will remain as healthy as ever despite the frailty of the physical body. When ego identification takes over, it begins to command basic survival instincts and turns them into tools of misery for us.

For instance, when hungry, instead of consuming enough food in order to satisfy our hunger, the ego will

convince us to eat far more than necessary. This is in response to some imagined future situations where food might be scarce or inaccessible to the ego. Creating such situations, either in the past or future, which guarantees misery, are the hallmarks of the ego.

If the ego is a 'mirage' and the problems it creates are not real, how valid can the solutions be? If the solutions are invalid, no problems are solved and the ego's suffering intensifies, leading to the creation of even more imagined problems. If we identify with the needs of the ego, we end up in this vicious circle, and the only outcome of this is an adversarial relationship with nature.

Every change, whether potential or real, is viewed with jaundiced eyes and this is in complete opposition to the way things really are. When living in such a warped reality, how can a person ever truly be free or prosperous? This sort of thinking is the root cause of all anxiety and other mental diseases. Anxiety and depression are not diseases, in fact.

They are symptoms of the real mental disease that is ego identification. When viewing life through the eyes of the ego, we cannot see the boundless possibilities available to us. It is a bit like glimpsing the ocean through a tiny crack in the wall. There is no possible way for us to begin to fathom the ocean's nature as long as we confine

ourselves to hiding behind this construct.

The challenge of questioning the ego lies in the fact that this form of thinking comes perfectly naturally to us. We experience the outside world through our bodies, and thus it is simple enough to ascribe meaning to it and to believe that the body is the true nature of ours. I am my body; I am what I do, and so on.

It never occurs to us to question all of this, and yet the path to spiritual liberation requires you to go beyond constructs. This is not to say that you should not want them. The problem occurs when you begin to attach importance to them and believe the lie that you are nothing without these materials or outside possessions.

Questioning your ego begins with examining the nature of your existence. For example, if you lost all of your possessions, would you still be you? Sure, existence might be unbearable, but will you become another person? If you change your name but don't change your behavior, do you change? If you drive another car, will you change?

Asking such questions will make you aware of the existence of an identity that is far beyond your ego, along with awareness of the existence of the ego. With this awareness, you are ready to begin the process of letting go of your need for the ego.

The Core of the Ego

If I had to summarize the reason for the ego's existence into one word, it would be fear. Fear rules the ego, but to simply leave it at that without an explanation would be to misunderstand it. The ego fears, above all, its destruction.

Just like a particularly inefficient vehicle that breaks down without going too far, the ego prevents us from fully realizing the nature of things around us and traveling on our spiritual path. The key to letting it go is twofold. First, recognize it for what it is, a mirage. Second, become aware of the fact that it does not exist. The more you go towards it, the more it will disappear and vanish. But, for this to happen, you must get closer to the fire.

The very act of recognition is a powerful one that will allow you to experience liberation. Think of it as shining a light in the darkness. The act of recognition is joined at the hip with learning to spot the characteristics of the ego so let's take a look at this.

Identity Drivers

The ego is mostly concerned with deriving an identity for itself thanks to its insecurity. This manifests as it trying to label something in a comparative fashion. Thus, experiences become good or bad, poor or rich, and so on. This

doesn't mean you do not pass judgment at all, but the problem arises when you begin to take them personally.

Let's say your flight was delayed horribly and you ended up reaching your destination thirty-six hours after you intended to arrive. Do you let this ruin your entire trip? Do you take the chance to regale everyone with how much you suffered? This is simply the ego deriving an identity for itself from the event.

Another key trait of the ego is its need to want things. The ego is characterized by want and is always after something shinier. This is a particularly insidious tactic since it can be difficult to separate the ego from the things you genuinely want as part of your purpose in life. It is perfectly fine to want more money or a better house and so on. It is attaching disappointment to the lack of it that is a trait of the ego and is where the trouble begins.

Taking things personally and acting from a sense of superiority or inferiority is another sign of ego. By distinguishing itself from the rest, the ego creates a distinct place for itself in what it sees as the scheme of things. Recall from the first chapter where we learned that liberation lies in recognizing that everything is one, and you'll see how mistaken the ego is and how counterproductive to your goals it can be.

Identification in and of itself is a characteristic of the ego. The idea that something defines you, be it your car or your wealth, and that without it you would be nothing is a sure shot way to obtaining misery. Identifying with yourself as someone who is particularly enlightened or smart or wise, is also a manifestation of the ego.

Does this mean you keep your mouth shut and feel guilty every time you say something smart? No, this is an egoistic construct as well since you're deliberately ignoring truth and carving an inferior complex for yourself. This is probably getting confusing but bear with me. My intention is to help you fully understand how the ego twists and turns your thoughts against you.

The minute you become aware of one characteristic, it props something else up in order to slip past you. View the ego as being the part of yourself that is clever, not wise, much like a child is of the world around them. It loves wearing a lot of hats and creating a new one every day, like a fancy dress competition.

One of the particularly strong hats the ego loves wearing has to do with our families. Often, once we move out and on with our lives, we change as people. However, visiting our families can often bring loads of misery because we tend to default back to who we were when we lived with them, an inferior self usually.

Recognition of this hat technique is a huge step in letting go of the ego's grip on you. When it comes to those we love, we cling onto these roles with particular fervor and play them out. Roles such as son, daughter, mother, wife, husband, father, and so on become central constructs in our lives, and there are few good arguments to get someone to reduce their reliance on such identities.

However, a few good arguments are all that exist. Freedom from misery is a particularly strong one. Whether it is a mother who becomes depressed when her child leaves home or a daughter who begins to act like a child when visiting her parents, all these roles do is bring us misery when we make them the central pillars of our lives.

The ego will put forward convincing arguments as to why you should not let go of these. After all, no one wants to be a bad parent or a bad child. Identifying the lie and catching yourself reacting to the ego will help you be able to let go of your need for it.

How to 'Detach' From the Ego

The most insidious trick that the ego pulls on you is to convince you that the protection it provides you with is necessary for your survival. The world is, after all, a big and bad place, and without this protective layer, you

would be lost. The ego's ultimate aim, as we have seen previously, is to create a sense of separation between itself and the rest of the world, and this creates an identity of the separate self.

Letting go of the ego, first of all, requires you to refrain from declaring war on it. By viewing it as the enemy, you're actually giving into it again since you're creating a 'me versus something' identity for yourself. A lot of people fall into this trap and end up spinning their wheels. The ego is a very clever trickster, and the way to defeat it is found in emptiness and ignorance.

Awareness of these games is great for what comes next, and the previous section has given you a number of pointers in this regard. Next, knowing some simple principles will help you to let go of your need for the ego and to mute the volume on the things it says.

Get To Know Yourself

What is your self-talk like? What are the things you regularly say to yourself? For the large majority of us, our self-talk is absolutely horrendous. We are many times more vicious towards ourselves than we would be with a stranger. Cloaking this sort of self-talk under the guise of 'self-improvement' is to play the ego's game.

As we've seen previously, vanity is not the only construct in which the ego satisfies itself. A sense of identity can be created out of inferiority as well. People often do this and practice things like false modesty, which is just their ego tricking them into believing that they are somehow superior to those around them by projecting inferiority.

Of course, asserting inferiority as an identity also applies. People deliberately put themselves in poor situations, such as abusive relationships, or wear their sufferings as a crown and thus create an identity for their egos to draw fuel from. By getting to know your self-talk and monitoring it for signs of the ego playing tricks, you're simply shining the light of awareness on it.

Much like how darkness is driven out by light, the ego can be minimized by realizing that it is there.

Your Voice Versus the Ego's Voice

So what does your true voice sound like? Odds are that you've heard this voice faintly because, for obvious reasons, it has become drowned out by the ego. Often when we are out in nature and view its creations, we fall silent and stand in awe of what lies before us. Similar feelings occur during truly miraculous moments, such as the birth of our children.

These moments remind us of our connection to the infinite and how the circle of life ties everything together. In these moments, the one thing that you will be profoundly aware of, besides your feelings, is the silence. Your brain falls absolutely silent and doesn't produce any words since the feeling cannot be described. After all, how can you describe the infinite?

Although words fall short in describing, they do not fall short in expressing. Language was invented for man as a tool of expression, yet many believe it to be a tool of definition. To define means to make definite, to grasp and keep, we live in a flowing present that is constantly changing and reforming itself. Words are no more than an expression of the infinite, and when we hold on to (believe) these words, we become ego-like and dense minded. These concepts of the mind should not be taken seriously but, at the same time, are extremely useful.

There are three kinds of thoughts that should arise for any needs:

1. A response to a present situation
2. To explore your life
3. To celebrate your life

If any other thought that should arise that does not correspond with this list, it may need questioning. A present situation may be an employer calling and asking if you can work overtime. You must make a decision and use thinking in order to move forward. If you fall into exploring your experience, you may find yourself communicating with others around you or asking yourself questions in your own mind like "Why am I transfixed at the beauty of this flower?" Lastly, celebrating an experience can also happen as an act of gratitude, internally or externally. For example; You are traveling and come across a beautiful place, you say "Wow, this place is breathtaking!" or when seeing another person and saying "She is so beautiful and kind". These are genuine thoughts that need no further questioning. They are not held and kept within the mind; they are expressed, felt, enjoyed, and released without attaching any sense of identity towards them like a rainbow-colored cloud passing by awareness.

Faith Towards Reality

Faith. This is a step that trips even the most ardent practitioners. The biggest reason for this is the lack of awareness of their current reality and misunderstanding one's belief about reality for the truth. Needless to say, the ego

is responsible for this belief. A lot of people draw solace from the fact that they are fighting and working hard to achieve their goals and aspirations.

This is the truth, but only half of it. People that enjoy their work and love every second of the 'hustle' are truly happy beings. But when someone makes or forces themselves to work and hustle, they create a false sense of happiness in their lives. They believe happiness comes after hard work. Thus, such people become happiness junkies and ignore their personalized reality. The fact is we must carry out faithful actions towards reality and feed our souls with passions and aspirations; otherwise, we are as Alan Watts said, "earning an earning". The real money will come to those who break through stereotypes and live a life of enjoyment and fulfillment. For they are vibrationally aligned with their lives, and a vibrationally aligned life is magnetic beyond compare.

The secret of the rich is in their faith. The wealthy own more than just shares; they are characterized by innate habits that allow them to succeed. For instance, Gary Vaynerchuck is a popular serial entrepreneur with a strong background in business. He claims that at age 13 he was making $3,000 a weekend selling baseball cards despite his horrible grades at school. He finds happiness in being an entrepreneur, and thus the ego is not much of a problem and doesn't get in the way of his life path. Ego-death is found in the faith of one's own true potential. They let themselves go.

Faith is a characteristic that ties to many other positive traits that few individuals carry. Where one is able to pursue his/her passion with no ties to the end goal. They flow with nature and adjust their course with purely God-like intentions. This aspect of reality is another reason why egos dissolve. The soul is jumping up and down gleaming through a person's being where the ego has no chance to interfere.

Remain Aware and Present

It's easy enough to say that you should be aware and that the present moment is all that you should be concerned with. The truth is that in practice, doing this will take time. Your mind is so used to turning to the ego thoughts for guidance in every situation that when you first realize it, it will seem odd and even otherworldly.

Feelings of discomfort are normal when you first do this. The key is to keep repeating the process of shining the light of awareness on your environment and keep brightening the light by hearing, seeing, tasting, smell-

ing, and touching the present moment. For your senses are of themselves present. The ego will eventually want to place an identity to this state, and that is okay, accept, and be aware of the ego and its efforts, and you will soon be free.

The worst thing to do is to try to crush it or adopt an adversarial attitude towards it. You're simply playing a game at which you're the novice against an expert player. There is no chance that you will win at this. Therefore, simply refuse to play. There's nothing the ego can do in response to this except whine and try to create illusionary problems like placing blames on others.

Awareness is what will rescue you in such situations and will ensure you remain focused on your presence. By deliberately doing this over and over, you will soon turn this into an automatic behavior, and your ego's voice will gradually reduce over time.

How To Prevent Being Drawn Back

Once you begin to shine awareness on the illusions of your ego, the first thing that happens is that the ego will become more apparent. You see, the ego does not want its problems to end. It wants to perpetuate them and thrive with the identity that those problems bring. You could

say that we are almost addicted to problems and the feelings that arise when such situations become present.

Here's the thing: You will constantly fluctuate between states of knowing and states of egoistic control. Some people become frustrated with this constant fluctuation, expecting an endpoint of some sort to manifest, but the truth is that there is no endpoint in store for us in a distant future. I'll say that again: There is no destination in ego-disillusionment, the place that you are in right now is the 'endpoint' and the 'starting point', or just the 'point' at which the ego dissolves. The problem ends by not engaging in the one that is present.

That previous statement is a scary thought to most people. Most likely, after reading that your so-called ego kicked in and started screaming that you do not want to be miserable for the rest of your life, and you need a respite from your current situation right now and so on. Despite knowing the ego's propensity for drama, this particular fact will be hard to accept.

In our world and environment, accepting that we do not know is seen as a sign of weakness. After all, we aim to remain in control of everything in our lives, and a lot of self-help gurus tell us to take responsibility and to take hold of our lives. However, true control lies in acceptance

and surrender. Just as we accept and surrender to the process of our blood circulation, our hair growth, and even the rising and setting of the sun.

We are free to make our plans, but ultimately, whatever will happen will happen. All we know for sure is that if we realize nonduality and see life's truth for what it is, everything will be balanced for us — assuming that we somehow know better than nature as to what is good for us. By clinging stubbornly onto life, we develop a habit of selfishness and ungratefulness.

People who are not ready to believe this will often find themselves pinging from one belief system to another. Today it is Buddhism, and tomorrow it is neuroscience. They might know intellectually that everything talks about the same concept, but their ego doesn't allow them to see this truth. Worse, the fear they feel makes their egos shield the truth from them.

Thus an identity of struggling against the ego is born. All of the mental noise going on inside your head are seen as imperfect. They are only imperfect because they are being resisted and fought against, which is simply damning the flow of thoughts.

Does this mean you should simply sit back and turn the other cheek at all times when life hits you? Of course

not. Truly letting go of your ego requires you to see that while you want the things you do, you'll still be fine if you don't get them. The ego tricks you into thinking that not achieving what you want automatically means you'll get what you don't want, and thus misery is guaranteed.

This way, it tricks you into building another identity based on your goals and your adherence to them. The only thing that does happen in this case is that you will suffocate them to death. Thus, let go. Detach yourself from absolutely needing your goals to come into reality. Allow yourself the golden opportunity for things to come into your life without the need for clinging.

Your goals are not you, no matter how amazing they might be. It is fine to want them but also acknowledge that there is an intelligence way beyond your comprehension, and you have the ability to surrender to it. As we saw in the previous chapter, this has the effect of removing the brakes inside your brain, and you end up achieving your goals and then some.

The old Buddhist story about the teacher imparting wisdom to the student using a cup is apt here. The teacher pours tea into a cup and keeps pouring until the tea overflows. The point that is being made is that a full cup cannot absorb new things. Our cups are full of

beliefs and images about who we are and what our lives ought to be like.

In order to absorb new information and to accept reality as it truly is, we need to empty our minds of this information and accept that we know nothing. 'Shoshin' in Japanese means 'beginner's mind', learn to carry this state within you. Maybe we do know some things, but even these might be wrong, who knows? Either way, the point of life is not to know everything. It is to go with the flow and accept the path of least resistance. Follow your intuition, do what you feel like doing, allow thoughts to emerge, allow thoughts to pass, and when you come across an obligation, surrender to it with positive intention.

The flow of least resistance will always take the path that is unknown to the mind, but it will always reach its destination in the end.

> *"True goodness is like water. Water's good for everything. It doesn't compete. It goes right to the low loathsome places, and so finds the way."*

This will be communicated to you as long as you keep shining awareness on your experiences and recognize its

flow. Experiencing the ego is no different than experiencing the sensation of a headache; they both come and go. You see, the beauty of letting go of your ego lies in the journey. The journey is the point, not the destination. Like with everything else in life, this is the case with the ego as well.

So sit back, relax, and surrender. Get out of your own way and let a greater intelligence handle your outcomes. Set your intentions, but don't become them. Strive towards them and do your best but remember that the ego's admonishment that your goals are the only good things in life and your only sources of happiness is false.

It is a long process and will seem tedious at times. However, that is the point of it all. It is only by traveling down the path of liberation that you will understand. Arriving at the destination without experiencing the path is a bit like tasting honey but not experiencing its sweetness.

Hence, surrender and allow yourself to be. You're perfectly fine.

CHAPTER 4

Experiencing Oneness

I've been going on about how everything is one and that there is no such thing as duality. However, duality can be so real to us because our world is full of contrasts. In fact, one of the best learning mechanisms that human beings have is contrast.

We often learn how to do a thing by learning how not to do it. Good and bad, right and wrong, up and down, everything exists as a duality for us. As a result, it can be tough to comprehend and even begin to understand the nature of oneness. So let's take a deep dive into this and see exactly what it's all about.

What is Oneness?

The logical place to start is to try to define what oneness is in the first place. While this may be logical, it is a pretty difficult place to start since, like most metaphysical realities, there is no way to quantify what this is. Oneness is not measurable in ways that make sense to us.

Oneness lies beyond our view of our world. I don't mean to say this in some extra-terrestrial sense but that the person who wishes to experience oneness needs to realize first what not to do. We've just seen how difficult it can be to let go of the ego, so constantly experiencing oneness is something that is like eating your favorite food every day. Sooner or later, your sense of taste will be numb to the flavors.

However, we do receive spikes from time to time. As if our senses decided to refine themselves and take in the lot. I've mentioned previously the feeling you experience when you see something in nature that is beyond compare and takes your breath away or the moment when you first saw your newborn child. These moments are when we are far removed from our egos and are made aware of a force that is beyond anything we can comprehend.

This is why oneness is impossible to describe in words. It is as if one is trying to outline a drop in the ocean and explain why its one with it. It has to be experienced. Oneness is understanding that all the duality we see around us is a part of the same universal thing. Like having our fingers look at each other. While the fingers may be separate, ultimately, everything belongs to the same body.

The ego is a huge barrier/bridge towards experiencing oneness, as you can imagine. The former puts its own need for an identity above all else; it forces us to turn against one another. Wars and conflicts are the results. The reasons for these conflicts make sense, but ultimately, on a universal level, there's nothing sensible about two fingers of the same hand fighting one another. The latter experiences the ego as oneness, for how can there be only one reality when we are trying to escape a 'dual' one? In other words, are we an ego pretending to be oneness or are we oneness pretending to be an ego?

A good realization to make towards experiencing oneness is to see all labels and to stop attaching them to experiences and materials. Recognize everything simply for what they are. It is your ego and intellect which places these fixated labels and hence draws all sorts of unnecessary analysis that result in suffering. You can't listen to

rock the same way by placing a rock next to your ear.

"Words and measures do not give life;
they merely symbolize it." -Alan Watts

Developing Oneness

While it is difficult to experience oneness as a steady stream of consciousness, aiming to achieve this state is missing the point. The beauty of experiencing oneness lies in its limitations. It is in this ego that you will realize the true nature of this world, or according to the Vedanta, maya originally meant 'device' and was described as the creative power of Brahman.

Like with everything else, immersing yourself in an environment that encourages the removal of the every day will help you expand 'common sense'. Transfixion, creativity, love, flow, beauty... all emerge when we can transcend what Michael Pollan calls the "been there and done that's of the adult mind" - in other words, jadedness. Being jaded by your experience is almost like being dead. Like, are you serious? Nothing impresses you because you feel like you've seen it all before, and you move through life with one leg dragging behind. The window closed, no

natural light gets in, Heaven fades into the clouds, and to me that's death. A sense of a new community helps us both serve and broaden our limitations. This is not to say that you should drop everything and join some group and go live in a forest together.

Instead, immerse yourself in activities and communicate with people who are seeking the same things. Some of them might be ahead of you and some behind. Either way, the fact that all of you are on the same journey is a wonderful thing. Books such as this one or those written by Eckhart Tolle, Dr. Joe Dispenza, and so on, are excellent tools and function as your guides along the path.

You can also utilize the power of contrast when it comes to learning about oneness. This seems an odd thing to say since contrast seems dual. So how can contrast help us understand oneness? Well, individuation manifests as a result of the diversity of oneness. It gives life color and depth. How can society function if everyone had the same face and everything the same name?

As we become more adept at our practice, the ego's voice diminishes and we experience greater levels of pure consciousness. This fluctuation between the two states helps us understand the nature of oneness better. Experiencing, with full awareness, a state of oscillation between

finite and infinite, is in itself a non-dual state that permeates everything around you. It is no coincidence that meditation is most effective when conducted as a Sangha, or in a community. This method leverages the best of both worlds.

Most people think that meditation is all about sitting on the floor, closing your eyes and observing your breath or chanting some mantra. This is a form of meditation, of course. However, not everyone has that kind of time on their hands to do what the Buddha did and sit under a tree and realize enlightenment. Meditation, at its core, is all about happiness. If you are considering meditating as another form of discipline or results-driven practice, you will have no effect on your long term well-being. When meditation is practiced as a way to dissolve the ego, you simply strengthen the illusion of a separate self. Meditation would be most beneficial when done as a form of play or enjoyment.

"...there is nothing wrong with meditating just to meditate, in the same way that you listen to music just for the music." - Alan Watts

Another form of meditation that many people enjoy is to incorporate awareness into every action you carry out.

When eating your food, really focus on what you're eating, how the food feels in your mouth, and what sensations you experience. When washing your hands, feel the water on your skin, and focus on how it makes you feel. Listen to the sounds you are hearing… you are listening to the present moment, no sound is in the past nor in the future, it is always now. Awareness is the mind's key to the oneness experience.

The problem lies in our minds 'ability' to switch thoughts so quickly that we believe we process multiple things at once. However, the mind is capable of entertaining just one thought at a time. By focusing on what is in front of you, you will be able to realize this truth and also dissolve time.

Time is what keeps the ego alive, and memory removes you from the present moment. By remaining consciously aware of what you are doing, you will be using the power of awareness to keep you grounded in the present moment. Consciousness also implies being aware of the repercussions of your actions.

By being aware of how your actions affect others, you will be connecting to an idea greater than yourself and removing your ego from the picture, as it is concerned with only itself. Observing and shifting your center of

gravity from self to the world will allow you to become conscious of the unity that exists within nature. Nature functions on the basis of laws which repeat themselves over and over in everything.

Seeing the pattern of this all and seeing how you are of this world is a great way to connect with the truth of your existence. Saying that God exists in everything and within you is just another way of saying that oneness connects all of us and that we're carved from the same rock, so to speak.

Lastly, love is both a method and a mark of your recognition of oneness. To live from a state of love is to live in accordance with the way the world functions. Living from love is a slightly different concept from 'being in love'. A lot of us associate love with romantic relationships or with familial ties, such as those between wife and husband or parent and children.

Living from a state of love implies a love for all things around you and is marked by a state of happiness and surrender. It also implies high levels of compassion for your fellow creatures and the recognition that everything is the same and everything is equally enlightened.

In short, living from love is simply living your life as you wish to live it, recognizing God or the infinite in

everything. Love is the ultimate marker of oneness since it causes you to live for something greater than yourself. Tales of romantic love often depict the state of being where both lovers sacrifice everything for the other, thus, they 'fall' in love rather than rise into it.

This is the supreme power of love. It removes you completely from yourself and causes you to acknowledge the greater existence of something else. To experience love is to experience oneness, via 'duality'.

The Connection Between All Things

One of the great mysteries of science is the lack of a theory connecting classical physics and quantum physics. This unified theory of everything has stumped the best brains out there and many attempts have been made to explain the disconnect. While nothing has been scientifically proven yet, certain interesting pieces of research have emerged.

The first conclusion that all scientists agree on is that classical physics is particularly bad at explaining the true nature of things. The universe is mostly composed of space. Not only is the universe composed of space but even atoms and subatomic particles are composed of empty space. In other words, despite appearing solid, the

truth is that the density of things around us, including our bodies, is extremely low.

The level of empty space is estimated to be close to 96%, both in terms of celestial bodies and our own. Classical physics can only explain about four percent of the stuff out there. It can explain how planets interact with one another but cannot explain the stuff that lies between them.

Classical physics explains this stuff away as being empty or antimatter with physical bodies being matter. However, with the rise of quantum physics, this explanation doesn't quite hold up. In other words, antimatter is just as real as matter is. Something even more mind-bending to consider is that since antimatter occupies such a large space in our reality, we are literally made of antimatter for the most part.

Space therefore exists in all of us and all around us. By its very nature, space can currently not be quantified or measured. Thus, the key to understanding universal oneness is to pay attention to ourselves, to turn within as spiritual teachings have often recommended.

Black Holes and Enlightenment

Why is dark matter or antimatter so difficult to study or comprehend? Well for starters, we can't see it. As every-

one knows from experience, it is quite difficult to comprehend something you cannot see. Much like the story of the three blind men who grasp different parts of an elephant and declare that to be the whole, we often don't know what we don't know when robbed of sight.

However, interplanetary physics does have a phenomenon which can explain antimatter and this is the black hole. We know of the existence of black holes thanks to the gravitational distortions that occur around it. We can even see black holes because of the way light bends and disappears into it. Thus, we can see black holes by the lack of light at their center.

Is it possible that black holes are what empty space is? Black holes often contain within them a particle called the singularity, which is where the force of the black hole emerges from. Given the amount of empty space within us, within our atomic structure, perhaps we're simply walking, talking black holes with singularities within us.

While this theory doesn't go all the way to explaining the disconnect between classical and quantum physics, it does have some connections to spirituality. For starters, spirituality is often concerned with discovering the truth within us and recognizing the reality that exists.

We often take this to signify exploring the material nature of ourselves, the quantifiable part. However, there

is just so much of us that is just empty space where there's nothing. It is precisely in the exploration of these spaces that truth emerges. Dark matter or antimatter simply signifies potential, space into which we can expand.

The truth of our existence as infinite beings, capable of whatever it is we wish to achieve lies right here, and this is precisely what spirituality has been teaching for all these years. To truly understand existence, you need to turn within and look inside. You truly are, after all, the center of the universe.

This is a pretty bold claim to make and requires some explanation. The truth is that in order to understand the nature of the world, we need to understand ourselves. Thus, by placing ourselves at the center of our consciousness, or the center of the universe, so to speak, we conduct our dialogue with the infinite.

Using the previous example of the three blind men touching different parts of an elephant, we are much like one of those blind men. It isn't a question of opening our eyes; we simply are not gifted with sight to begin with. All spiritual practices are about understanding the portion of the universe (elephant) that has been gifted to you.

Feeling the trunk of the elephant and thinking it to be the entire elephant and even worse, going to war with

the other person who insists the tail is the entire elephant is precisely what we currently do, by insisting that our point of view is the only true method. Religion, generally speaking, has been corrupted in this manner through a variety of practices and prescriptions that simply do not make any sense.

This is why it is necessary to both turn inward and acknowledge the presence of antimatter, or nothing, within yourself. Explore the spaces. It helps us understand the presence of the infinite and the possibility that something far more intelligent exists. After all, if our physical form is only 4% of our entire being, it stands to reason that something bigger can potentially exist.

Ultimately it is important to understand that you are merely made from or a participant of the universe. You are its entirety. By journeying inward, you get to experience the universe as it stands. For us as human beings, understanding this small portion is more than enough to realize enlightenment.

Ultimately, enlightenment is all about realizing our presence as made up of the whole process. It is understanding that the other person claiming the tail of the elephant as the only reality is simply holding a different feature of the same thing and that both of you are experiencing different facets of the same reality.

Thus, there is no absolute truth or lie. This doesn't mean to say that you should reject facts outright. Just that, it is important to differentiate between opinion and fact. This particular point has been ignored to a large extent, and people claim all sorts of 'facts' that are really opinions and force them on others, spreading misinformation.

Doing this is simply the act of the ego. People who indulge in this sort of behavior usually try to force their points of view onto others and don't recognize that the other point of view has a right to exist. While some of the conclusions of the counterpoint of view might be wrong and unscientific, this does not invalidate the entire point of view. It is just a reality that we cannot see.

Science and spirituality are merely tools of dialogue between us and the universe. It is how we explore our little bit and understand the true nature of reality, even if we don't comprehend the entire nature of it. The most powerful aspect of looking at things this way is that you can realize that you are not only made of truth and creation, but you are a creator yourself.

After all, how you choose to view the world is what the nature of your reality will be. Is it any surprise then, that you are perfectly free to manifest whatever it is that you

want in your life? Ultimately, everything is connected. We do not know the scientific or even the spiritual mechanism by which the movement of atoms explains the movement of celestial bodies.

All we know is that we need to conduct a dialogue and the best way to conduct it is to turn within because that is where truth lies.

Nonduality

By now, I've been talking of nonduality for a long time and it is important to clarify a few things. First, the nature of dialogue with regards to nonduality often takes a comparative tone that is of duality versus nonduality. While this is an effective learning tool at the start, as you understand these concepts better, it does not serve your purpose to cling onto this adversarial view of things.

This is simply a form of classifying, which will soon involve the ego, and we've seen how damaging that can be. The truth is that nonduality is reality. Everything else you heap on top of it is simply a veil that obscures it. Therefore, there is no concept of trying to adopt a nondual view of the world or of trying to accept something. How can you accept something you already are?

Well, the key is to allow it to express itself. Much like how you need to allow your brain to move forward with its

plans instead of pumping the brakes via your mental constructs, you need to allow yourself to simply exist. Most
people who pick up a book of this kind are searching for
something. There is a hole within, whether you realize it
or not and there is a desire to fill this hole with something.

Thus, liberation and enlightenment or whatever you
want to call it becomes a holy grail of sorts. Looking at
these objectives in this manner is to miss the true nature
of reality. You are already an enlightened being. You simply need to allow it to shine through. Accepting and realizing your nonduality is a step in this process, and even
this is simply a case of allowing it to come forth.

If allowing is the key to happiness, then what is the
key to suffering? Well, not allowing or blocking who
you truly are causes suffering. The various truths of your
existence have been expanded upon previously. The one
aspect of this I haven't touched upon as yet is the relationship of your existence with time. We are slaves to
time if you look at how we live our lives.

We eat, sleep, play, and work according to the clock.
We even get paid according to the clock; most of us do
anyway. What we do not realize is that our ego has again
taken something good and warped it into something
negative to the point that we don't recognize it anymore.

Presence and Nonduality

What is the strongest relationship in your life? Is it with your spouse? Your parents? Your children? Well, all of these are the wrong answers, no matter how great your interpersonal relationships are. The strongest relationship in your life is between you and the present moment. In fact, in this relationship you have no choice whatsoever, you cannot walk away from it and if you try your efforts will only cause unhappiness.

The present moment is what contains everything. All that will happen to you in the future is determined by what you do right now. All the consequences of your past actions have led you to this moment right now. The old Chinese proverb about the current moment being a gift and hence being called the present is quite apt when viewed in this manner.

Yet, the biggest struggle we face in our lives is to try and escape the present. We imagine futures that are far better than this one or revisit and mentally fix prior mistakes. We do almost everything to not be present and distract ourselves with worldly pleasures. We would rather slowly have our brain wither away watching mindless television than sit quietly with ourselves!

This flitting back and forth in time is an egoistic construct. The ego seeks to survive from this time traveling and in the process completely warps what Eckhart Tolle calls 'clock time'. Clock time is a wonderful thing because it helps us organize our present moments into productive blocks.

The idea is that by doing so, we achieve more and organize ourselves better. However, the ego takes clock time and turns it into something unrecognizable. All of a sudden we need to achieve goals by a certain point in time or else we label ourselves failures. We need to become liberated by a certain point, or else the entire spiritual journey is a waste.

This is framing of time in a dualist perspective. Dividing time into past and future segments, and considering them as real segments of time is to turn your cheek on reality. Does this mean you should not set goals or visualize what it is you wish to manifest? Hardly. As described before, visualize and feel good about your future goals but recognize that you as a person will not change or become worse if this goal isn't hit exactly as you want it.

If you believe in an unjust world, you'll think of not achieving your goals as a bad outcome. If you understand the truth of the world, you'll understand that the

lack of your desired outcome doesn't imply a negative result for you. Thinking in solely positive or negative outcomes is to adopt a dualist and unbalanced perspective of the world.

The only true moment is the present. And any form of future vision cannot be real if you are unable to live fully present. Time is nondual. Aside from the present, nothing else exists, and this is why it is of massive importance that you use it wisely. At this point, you might be thinking that the solution to this predicament is to seek to be more present. This is wrong as well. Seeking also implies a dualist perspective of the world.

Seeking implies that the current situation is worse than some other imagined one. The truth is that your existence is what it is. It doesn't say anything about you. Instead of seeking, allow presence to come to you by setting your intention to be present and not making anything as a means for an end like brushing your teeth, or working out at the gym.

You will not attain presence by grasping for it. It will come when it needs to. Remember how we learned that to cling onto what you want is to strangle it to death? Well, the same principle applies here. Presence is really about discovering your reality, or should I say, rediscovering it.

Your future lies right here, right now in your hands. So does your past. Everything that will ever happen to you is happening right now. So let go of your ego's needs by recognizing its presence and simply do what you're doing right now, well. You see, nonduality exists with you right now.

You don't need to go anywhere in order to seek it. It is your truth. You are made of something intelligent and by giving in to your ego's needs to forge an identity, you're simply trying to separate yourself from the whole. This makes absolutely no sense. It is like one finger of yours deciding that it is a body in and of itself and trying to separate itself from you.

Needless to say, no matter how much that finger desires it, it isn't leaving your whole body unless you decide to intervene in some manner. Similarly, your ego's efforts to separate itself will only result in misery. Its dualist manner of thought brings suffering, and allowing yourself to surrender to the whole and recognize the nondual nature of your existence is the key to happiness.

CHAPTER 5

The Art of Adaptation

As human beings, we have some very powerful survival tools within us. These tools are present within us, thanks to evolution or the kindness of God, depending on whether your viewpoint is scientific or spiritual. These gifts help us adapt and live better lives in a world that is always changing.

Unfortunately, these natural instincts get curbed for a variety of reasons and following the words of these limiting thoughts leads to more trouble. Much like when you learned about the ego, awareness is the first step to removing these limiting beliefs from existence.

What is the Superego?

Well, you've learned about the ego. Now, you'll learn about the superego. There's no need to be alarmed though. The superego isn't some villain like what you'd face in a video game. Unlike the ego, the superego is actually a benevolent pattern of thought and is largely looking out for you, even if its claims are misguided.

In order to experience a life of joy and wellbeing, it is essential for you to recognize the superego and the effects it has on you. You need to recognize its voice and the particular admonishments it chooses to unleash on you in particular situations. The superego is also referred to sometimes as a false God. The reason for this is that often the superego presents itself as intuition and it can be confusing to separate the voice of intuition from the superego.

This is especially true if you suffer from anxiety and tend to overthink things. There are some key differences between the two, which I'll list later in this section. First, we need to understand where the superego comes from. Much like everything else in your life, the seeds of the superego are sown in our childhood.

During this time, we are completely helpless and rely on our parents or guardians for everything. We innately realize this and unquestioningly follow whatever they tell us. Thus, the basic pattern of our belief system is born. What's funny to think about is that a lot of these beliefs have simply been handed down through generations. Your mother learned about raising a child from your grandparents and them from their parents and so on. Religious belief is a good example of this.

Often, children are not presented with a choice of religion and simply follow whatever religion their parents follow. This is not done maliciously on the parents' part, but you must understand that no human being is perfect. Every person transfers some of their neuroses onto their children, and this is how it has always been.

This does not mean that you are a slave to what your parents believed. You are perfectly able and capable of breaking free from this cycle. However, doing so is far from straightforward.

Formation of the Superego

The superego is simply a collection of the dos and don'ts that your peers drilled into you when you were a child. Think back to when you flouted some of the rules in

your house. Perhaps you jumped onto the couch when your parents were concentrating on something and got shouted at.

As kids, we unquestioningly accept everything that our parents and teachers tell us, thanks to us being 'helpless'. This dynamic changes as we grow up and develop our consciousness. We go from being playful, happy, and a little annoying, to being compressed by how others react. The child does not know he is being annoying until someone overreacts to his childlike nature, causing him to tense up and hide away this aspect of his personality. As we grow, we reveal glimpses of this playfulness and happiness. However, our minds remain deeply influenced by how our peers react to anything that we do, no matter how rebellious we are as teenagers.

If we choose to pursue some field of interest that our parents disapprove of, you can bet that tension will arise from you stepping out of their worldview. Your guilt will be constantly restimulated by an inner voice of "Am I doing the right thing". The voice in your head keeps you 'safe' from stepping out of bounce to keep the game in play.

This parent voice eventually needs to be reconciled with the reality around you because if it isn't, it forms

a shield between you and the world. A poverty mindset is a prime example of this happening. The children of poor families usually end up being poor. Why is this? You could argue that poor children are denied the same level of opportunities that children from richer households are exposed to.

However, often people who grew up poor and then became rich find it difficult to reconcile their feelings of guilt with regard to money. If not addressed, a lot of them tend to lose this money or keep only a portion of it. It's almost as if there's a financial thermostat within them that lets them know that a certain amount of wealth is comfortable and not more.

Logically, we often know when this is happening. Once you're aware even a little of this voice, it is easy to logically understand that this voice is wrong. However, we still unconsciously follow its advice. Why? Well, this is simply the Pavlovian instinct we developed as children.

If your parents told you not to do something, you didn't do it period. If you did, there would have been some sort of negative experience in store for us. We automatically assumed that they were right and we were wrong and didn't think twice about not doing what they wanted. This pattern holds largely throughout childhood.

During the teenage years we are still influenced by our parents' words even if we do not follow them. Some people continue to rebel against what their caregivers told them to do well into adulthood and every time the superego pipes up with some advice, they go out and do the exact opposite even if it is harmful for them.

Realities of Our Life Path

The struggle with our superego causes us to shut ourselves away from what is actually happening around us. To put it bluntly, we lose our objectivity in evaluating circumstances and lose our connection with the part of our brain that has the ability to reason and feel its way out of the situation we're in.

The superego is just another wall, much like the ego is, and these limiting beliefs about yourself will convince you of a reality that is counter to the truth. The key thing to recognize is that unlike the ego, which is seeking to develop its own identity and to somehow dissociate itself from reality, the superego's aim is not to harm you and neither is it self-serving.

Much like your parents, its ultimate aim is to help you. Often your parents just didn't know any better and were just looking out for you when they told you cer-

tain things. The paramount concern of this voice is your safety and therefore, it will almost certainly discourage you from doing anything even remotely risky.

Life however doesn't quite work that way, does it? All of us know that to earn a reward we need to run risks. Thus, no matter how well-intentioned the advice is, the superego runs counter to our goals and aims. Awareness is the starting point of shutting down the superego. Along with awareness, constant emphasis on doing the thing the superego warns you against also leads to it piping down. The reason for this is biological.

Your brain is essentially one giant neural network, with networks of neurons crisscrossing everywhere. When a particular belief pattern presents itself in your thoughts, this is simply a neural network lighting up. The stronger the neural network is, the more it lights up, and in turn, the stronger it becomes.

Deactivating this harmful neural network requires you to install a new network and there's no way to do this except through brute force repetition. When you become aware that a certain belief is asserting itself, you're essentially activating a counter network. However, merely activating it isn't enough.

At the end of the day, the network that is stronger is going to assert itself. So your job is to make sure that this new network lights up as much as possible. Repeatedly thinking in the new pattern, by realizing that your old beliefs are wrong and that you do know that this new path is good for you is the way to strengthen the new network and deactivate the old one.

Confusing Anxiety with Intuition

Intuition is the voice of the infinite expressing through you and the closer you stick to the real path of life, the more you'll hear its voice. Over time, you will get used to its vagaries and the manner in which it speaks to you. Anxiety on the other hand is a mental construct and rises from the ego or the superego.

I might as well say this right now: no matter how many pointers I give you, you're likely to confuse the two voices. This is because we're so used to listening to the voice of anxiety that we automatically pay heed to what it says. Further compounding the difficulty at first is that your intuition is equally likely to warn you of negative consequences as it is of positive ones.

Generally speaking, there are some things you can watch out for. Intuition's voice, whether it is warning you

of negative consequences, will always result in positive results. What I mean to say is that if you fail to listen to your intuition or don't do something to the best of your abilities, your intuition will speak up and warn you. If you ignore this voice, it will result in a negative feeling.

However, the intention of the voice is to bring about positive results. Once you carry out what the voice tells you to do, you'll feel lighter and happier knowing that you've done things correctly. Anxiety is the opposite. First off, it is never positive and doing what it tells you to do will result in your feeling even more anxious and sad.

The voice of intuition is often inclusive and subtle, while anxiety tends to place you in a loud yet lonely state. Your intuition never speaks in absolutes or in extreme tones. It never tells you that doing something is the best possible thing or the worst. That sort of language is anxiety or the superego talking.

Feeling your way through these voices is the key to understanding the differences and it isn't easy to put words to emotions as you know. Allow yourself to make mistakes. Thinking that you need to immediately know the differences between the two is the ego talking, so ignore it. Take your time getting to know your ego, superego, and intuition and know that you will spot the differences soon enough.

Relationships

Relationships are a fertile topic, aren't they? More than anything else, our relationships have the ability to harm us or improve our lives beyond compare. Given these sorts of stakes, is it any wonder than we cling onto them so much that we turn them into prime sources of misery for ourselves and our partners?

A lot of us unwittingly turn our relationships into wells of misery by becoming far too dependent on them, thus, creating an independent relationship. This is often due to us not realizing our own true nature or due to us feeling a hole that needs to be filled within. When we become conscious of this gap within us, our first instinct is to reach for something outside of us to fill it.

We expect another person to fill this gap and complete us somehow. Hollywood doesn't help the cause with its constant depictions of obsessive and narcissistic love, where one partner has to sacrifice everything in order to prove to the others that they do indeed love them. In reality, this kind of relationship creates feelings of inferiority that take up a lot of energy to sustain. The relationship becomes tense and the couples dissonant.

True unconditional love is never about sacrifice or having to deny our basic natures. If anything, it is the direct opposite. The love that most of us follow in failed relationships is egotistical love. This love springs from the ego and is concerned first and foremost with defining an identity for ourselves via the relationship.

This sort of love always turns unhealthy because the expectations are extremely unrealistic. I mean, how on earth can another person ever make you whole? It is impossible. We still strive to make this a reality and do our best to control the behavior of the person we're in a relationship with. Pretty soon, before we realize it, we're behaving like the bad guy.

Codependency in relationships works the other way as well. It isn't necessary that you be the one who is the controlling one, often people who lack a sense of identity place themselves in the position of being abused and controlled. It is easy to see why such a person would do this if you see if from their ego's point of view. There is no more sympathetic position than this to forge an identity with.

Often the superego convinces people to stick with abusive and unfulfilling relationships. This might be due to the pattern established by their parents and loved ones when they grew up. They might be the most successful

and rational person, but when it comes to relationships, they behave like a lamb lost in the woods.

The first thing to realize is that the universe exists in a state of balance. Everything that strays too far away from the middle path is subject to 'balancing forces' as Vadim Zeland terms it. The impact of these forces is almost always negative. By placing too much significance on the relationship to try to forge an identity, all you're doing is opening yourself up to the universe to push the relationship further away from yourself.

If the relationship is far too important in your mind, the universe will do its best to reduce its importance with the least amount of energy expenditure. It will do this by making it even more unfulfilling for you and thus you will be caught in a vicious circle of bad and worsening relationships. Understanding the origin of your patterns, via your superego, and then realizing that your identity is in your hands is the first step you need to take to restore balance.

True love is not about you at all. It is entirely unconditional. This love is not restrictive or controlling but is about growth. Think of it as wanting someone but not needing them. After all, you are secure in knowing who you are, warts and all, and you realize that this doesn't make you inferior or superior to the other person. You're both imperfect and that's what makes your relationship perfect.

Relationships based on unconditional love are ultimately a way of realizing the nonduality in this universe via your individual differences. You both belong to the same soul, and your relationship is just a reflection of this. Your partner is not responsible for your shortcomings, and neither are they responsible for fixing them.

Sure, they will help but ultimately it is you who needs to do the legwork and take care of yourself. You also recognize that you are not responsible for each other's happiness. If you rely on the relationship to make you happy, this is a major indication that your love is coming from the ego and not from the soul. True love that emanates from the soul is not about compensating for anything. It is about supporting your partner in what is best for them, even if it means that they need to leave you.

It is in a word, selfless. Beware the trap of trying to build an identity by aiming for this selfless sort of love since this is just the ego trying to trick you.

Adapting to Psychological Time and Clock Time

I have briefly mentioned Eckhart Tolle's notion of clock time versus psychological time. Clock time is simply the

time that is on your clock. It has no meaning beyond the blocks you divide it into in order to be more productive throughout your day. Psychological time is perhaps the biggest cause of anxiety and other negative patterns in our lives.

A lot of the problems we have in life result from an imperfect response to change. We seek to provide ourselves with security and banish the possibility of chaos and unpredictability. However, life itself is unpredictable. There is no way we can predict with any accuracy what is going to happen tomorrow, no matter how many astrologers or psychics claim to do so.

By wanting and clinging to this facade of wanting to end unpredictability, we inadvertently set ourselves up for failure to adapt because we're building a barrier between ourselves and life. How can you adapt to change when you seek to stop it? It is impossible. As much sense as this makes logically, we do not follow this intuitively.

The building of barriers to life causes us to start believing in the fallacy of time. Here's the thing: Time is not real. The present moment cannot be measured to any degree, before you even start to measure, it's already gone. Time is made up. Have you ever lost yourself in a task that you loved? Have you ever sat through a sleep-induc-

ing lecture? What was your perception of time in both cases? Despite whatever your clock told you the duration of these events were, there is no doubt that one of them was longer than the other.

Clock time simply tells you the time that has elapsed; that's it. The ego takes clock time and applies it to all sorts of things to build a story about itself. Thus, your goals need to be achieved by the age of 30. If you're not married by the age of 32, you're a failure and so on. Judgment is derived from the outcomes of clock time and we terrorize ourselves with these images.

This is what psychological time is. Under this false construct, we convince ourselves to make decisions that are detrimental to our happiness. If we have to get married by the age of 32, what does it matter who we get married to? Freeing yourself from the construct of time is a huge step towards liberating yourself.

This doesn't mean you trash all the clocks in your home. Instead, recognize that clocks are merely ways of organizing your day. They don't have any hold upon you and you can choose to reorganize yourself at will. Do not extend clock time beyond its intended use. Any time you feel the ego asserting its need for an identity by attaching importance to the clock, remind yourself that psychological time is untrue.

Science has proved that time is malleable. Via Einstein's theory of relativity, we know for sure that time is perceived differently under different circumstances. We are perhaps the only species on the planet who use something false to torture ourselves despite knowing that it isn't real. Whatever you might say about this, you have to admit this is conclusive proof of how marvelous our brains are!

All psychological unease begins with this imperfect understanding of time and using it to build walls around us. Mental disease is just a symptom of a disconnect from reality. People who suffer from such afflictions have been led by their egos to believe that the world is a dangerous place, thanks to its unpredictability.

Time offers a seemingly easy solution to this unpredictability because the ego thinks that if it fixes starting and ending points to certain tasks, it is in control. Of course, nothing of the sort is true. Time, in reality, is free-flowing and never stops. Every moment is the present one and is constantly in motion. Our futures and pasts reside right now and nothing is real except what is happening right now.

This is a difficult thing for the ego to understand because if reality isn't fixed, how on earth is it supposed

to draw a definite identity? This would be like trying to write on flowing water. Hence, it tries to build a dam and pretend it's in control. When the inevitable flood happens, we then run around blaming the water and not the construct that caused the flood. Who are we in the absence of memory? Who are we with the absence of resistance? Who are we in the absence of an ego?

Freedom from Mental Unease

The nature of life is flow. To enter the flow state is to let go of your ego and to simply run with what comes, trusting that you will be taken care of. This is why surrender and trusting your intuition are such important things to do if you wish to liberate yourself.

The ego cannot exist in harmony and your act of surrender will do more to dissolve it than anything else. True strength lies in vulnerability, not in the number of objects you possess.

The ego needs constant validation and feedback and this damages the nature of our relationships. It cuts us off from truth by building walls and damaging our relationship with time. The truth is that human beings, and every life form on this planet, have powerful adaptation systems to enable them to succeed in this life.

As Dr. Maxwell Maltz proved in his book Psycho Cybernetics, every living creature has an automatic mechanism that works in the present moment to enable it to make the best decision for itself. A newborn baby does not need to be told that it needs to eat or breathe to survive. When it is hungry, the baby cries for food, using the only means of communication available to it.

We innately know what to do and how to achieve what we want. It's just not apparent to us in the moment. Our adaptation abilities point us in the direction we need to take. Biologically, this manifests as our ability to evolve as a species over thousands of years. Our brains are learning machines and much like a missile that finds its target, it needs negative feedback to know what not to do.

This is why mistakes are important. They're simply an example of how not to do things, as Edison said. Learning from mistakes is a part of your ability to adapt, and people stifle this because of the ego's message that mistakes are something inferior people do. We thus cut ourselves away from life and still expect to perform at our best.

In order to free ourselves from mental unease, we need to open ourselves entirely to the emotion that we're feeling. This is a tough thing to do. Our default reaction is to shut ourselves away from the pain for understandable

reasons. However, shutting yourself away only makes things worse as the pain simmers underneath, ready to explode at inopportune moments.

Acknowledging and merging with the reality of what you're feeling will automatically dissolve the sensation of it, you are freeing yourself from the grip of anxiety and depression. Your brain will be racing ahead to all sorts of scary images and it will take the combined force of your intention and knowledge (the various things we're talking about in this book) to slow it down and to detach from it.

Logically, this makes sense to all of us but putting it into action is another thing entirely. The key is to repeat the helpful action as much as possible and to keep reinforcing new knowledge all the time. Be aware of when your old patterns assert themselves and weaken them by reminding yourself of the harm they cause.

Little by little, your adaptive ability will come to the forefront and you will partake in the gift that is life.

CHAPTER 6

The Future of Today's World - Stepping Forward into the Past

The rate of change in our world these days can cause your head to spin. Human beings are perhaps the worst when it comes to adapting to change. You see, animals and other beings that have lower levels of consciousness don't really have a choice when it comes to what they want to do.

Nature has programmed them with a few preset patterns and these patterns are remarkably robust when it comes to adapting to change. Migration is a good example of this. Human beings have a brain that is capable of creation and this causes a problem when it comes to change.

The irony is that this is perhaps the first time in history where we're fully realizing our inability to adapt to the

change we ourselves are creating. The solution to dealing with the speed of change, paradoxically, lies in the past.

Exponential and Linear Growth

Think of a task or a project that you completed recently. You mapped out the steps you needed to carry out during the planning stage and probably had mile markers which helped you figure out your rate of progress and how far or close to your ultimate goal you were. This is a prime example of linear thought processes.

A linear process places a huge premium on steady progress. We even think of our goals as a journey where we take a step at a time and reach destinations along the way which let us know where we are. This is how our world is currently set up, and this is how we've been raised as well. In today's society, we attend school, we then look forward to moving on to the next grade level until we finally begin to place expectations of making it to college and so on. After college, we are thrown out of a system and into another more complex and unpredictable system, which causes us to feel isolated and alone in some hopes of 'future' salvation. We were being taught to place hopes and dreams in the future rather than the present.

This model of thinking exists simply because it has worked well throughout human history. It has enabled us to make steady progress over time but as we kept making progress, a new reality began asserting itself, slowly but surely, and has now become an eventuality. This new reality is the exponential growth model or the exponential thought model.

Exponential Patterns

Neils Bohr (remember him?) was one of the first scientists to remark that the nature of technological change is exponential and not linear. An exponential curve by nature is one that moves slowly in the beginning and then gathers steam at rates that seem mind-boggling. Compound interest is an example of an exponential curve.

If you set aside $1000 in an account that pays you interest of 20% yearly, and you don't touch it, what's going to happen to it over time? Well, at the ten-year mark, you're going to have a grand total of $6191.74 in it. Not much is it? Well, ten years might be too short for this, so let's look at what our account balance is at the end of thirty years. At the thirty-year mark, we have $237, 376.61 in the account.

This is a lot more, but honestly, if you hold a regular job for twenty years and have no debt, by the thirty-year mark you would have probably accumulated savings equal to this amount. So it isn't very impressive really. Let's extend it further to the fifty-year mark and see what happens. Well, something funny has happened in the twenty years in between.

The account balance now reads $9,100,438! That's almost ten million dollars. In the space of twenty years, you've gone from having less than a quarter of a million to having close to ten million. During the first thirty years, you plodded along from around ten thousand to two hundred thousand so this sort of growth is surprising to say the least.

Well, this is what exponential growth is. The tiniest of changes made in the beginning have an outsized impact on the end. Let's say we invested $2000 instead of $1000 at the start. How much do we have at the end of fifty years? We've doubled our initial investment so you'd expect a change of at least that much. Well, the final amount is $18,200,876. That's an additional $200,876 that you receive by investing the additional $1000 over and above the doubled amount. It's like free money!

Our brains are singularly incapable of comprehending this sort of growth. We simply don't think of $1000 as costing us close to $9,000,000 in fifty years. We probably look at the additional $1000 investment as better saved for a down payment on a house or a car. Yet the truth is that nature is exponential.

Look at basic natural processes like evolution and reproduction. Everything works on the principle of geometric progression, which is to say that things grow exponentially. Our brains though, work on the basis of an arithmetic progression. Organizations are slowly coming to terms with the realities of exponential growth and its implications for investment.

Technology stands at a tipping point where it is ready to disrupt everything in our lives. Biotechnology, for so long the domain of stem cell researchers and the ensuing debate about the ethics of it, is now poised to take a leap far beyond what our minds can comprehend. DNA is simply blocks of code.

The crazy thing about all of this is that the faster technology advances, the more its solutions wind up mimicking natural patterns. Take the emergence of AI for example. AI research has been around since the 90s and for the longest time, your $1000 invested into it would

have seemed like dead money. Nothing much would have happened to it.

Do you think you'll say the same thing fifty years from now? We've gone within a lifetime of having no cell phones to having pocket-sized computers, which are more powerful than the computer that sent men to the moon for the first time. How much longer will it be before the smartphone becomes a part of us, like an implant?

We naturally resist this because our brain cannot comprehend the pace of change. We can calculate simple interest but compound interest throws us into confusion. Now, I'm not advocating that you start inserting implants into yourself but that you need to recognize that part of getting back to reality is to adopt an exponential thought process and to see that it exists all around you.

It seems odd to say this, but the best way to align technology and our existence is to invest more in our own thought processes. This is exactly what companies are doing these days by hiring philosophers who have a propensity to think about change in a better way. This is exactly why Mark Cuban says that the most important college degree moving forward will be in liberal arts since people need to learn how to think.

Whether you agree with this assessment or not, you do need to open your eyes to this reality instead of cling-

ing to a version of reality that you're used to. The linear world is simply a mental view that helps you focus but at the same time is keeping you in the dark. Begin to see the potential of an exponential world and you'll understand why it is easy to overestimate what you'll do in a day and underestimate what you'll do in a year, as Bill Gates says.

Why does our brain resist change and the exponential view so strongly? Well, its greatest strength is its greatest weakness in this case. Our brain is capable of creating its own reality. This leads us to believe that any obstacle that changes places in our path can be overcome by using existing thought patterns. This thought pattern holds true during our lives due to the fact that a lot of obstacles we encounter have been placed there by ourselves due to ignorance.

This ignorance comes from a selective mindset, also termed as 'spotlight consciousness' from the famous philosopher Alan Watts. He claims that humans have a very selective way to sense their environments, for example; light is not pure light, it is light/darkness. sound is not sound; it is sound/silence. Same goes for causes and effects; they are one of the same. We have adopted a narrowed perception of the world. He goes on to say:

"But a scanning process that observes the world bit by bit soon persuades its user that the world is a great collection of bits, and these he calls separate things or events. We often say that you can only think of one thing at a time. The truth is that in looking at the world bit by bit, we convince ourselves that it consists of separate things, and so give ourselves the problem of how these things are connected and how they cause and effect each other. The problem would never have arisen if we had been aware that it was just our way of looking at the world which had chopped it up into separate bits, things, events, causes, and effects"

(More details found in: "The Book: On the Taboo Against Knowing Who You Are")

Creating such a habit makes it difficult to merge with such an exponential world. Where before the internet we would be absorbing bits of information in a steady dose, we are now overdosing on an infinite number of bits. There is no wonder there is such confusion and anxiety around overcoming obstacles and choosing what is best for us. Because we sincerely don't know what to do. It is like placing dog treats all around a puppy; he'll run in circles, not knowing where to start.

Overcoming man-made obstacles requires creative solutions but in order to overcome natural obstacles and obstacles that result from an unwillingness to move with nature cannot be overcome in this manner. Creating a solution to maintain an inefficient way of living will simply place you in a stressful existence. Think of it as stubbornly flowing against the current.

You can be the strongest swimmer in the world but eventually, you will tire and have to give in. Thus, changing the way you view the world and viewing it with humility is the key to adapting to change. As we discussed in the previous chapter, recognition of a greater intelligence and surrender helps you overcome these challenges with ease.

Ancient Wisdom

The notion of a greater intelligence is of course par for the course when studying ancient philosophy and religion. The Tao Te Ching offers remarkable insight into dealing with the nature of exponential change, despite being written in what we think of as technologically primitive times.

The Tao Te Ching is an almost incomprehensible piece of work when viewed in linear terms. Throughout our lives, we've been conditioned to think that the way

to a successful and fruitful life is to put in a lot of hard work and then wait for the rewards to come automatically. Recall how your school days went by and how the modern workplace is setup if you're an employee working at a job.

The Tao, roughly translated to mean 'The Way', recommends Wu-Wei (effortless action) as the means to a successful life. It is a circular piece of philosophy and applies equally well as a political construct. Right at the start of this work, we are warned that the Tao has no name. To name something is to give it form and the Tao is formless.

Thus, right from the start begins a process of head scratching which continues throughout the book. The meaning of the first few lines is really to remind us of the limitations of the constructs we've created for ourselves. Things like time, language and action are used to serve our needs in this world.

However, how can one understand things outside of this world by using this world's language? That would be akin to trying to explain what a highway is to an ant using English or some human language. Ultimately the connection to the next world is via our emotions, and our hearts are at the center of this communication.

A lot of ancient philosophies explain the connection of the heart to the divine in different ways but ultimately agree on it being the center of everything. The brain is the machine that powers our lives on this planet, but communication and divine assistance arrive via the heart. By giving the brain too much importance, we ignore the words of the heart and shut ourselves away.

The meridian system and the chakra centers have been used to explain the flow of energy within us, according to ancient texts originating in the Indian subcontinent. A series of seven chakras starting from the navel to the top of the head signifies both the obstacles to divine energy as well as ways to remove blocks. While a lot of this literature is hijacked these days to sell crystals and gemstones, the original texts make a clear connection between the acceptance of reality and the flow of energy.

When speaking of attaining the flow state and adopting the path of least resistance, this is exactly what I'm referring to. Enlightenment is not a case of learning new things but of forgetting what we know to remember what we don't know. We know all of this when we're born but along the way adopt the constructs of the world we live in.

Merging with this world is a huge step in attaining liberation. This merging process is exponential. It begins

and ends with awareness. The objects you see and the space between them is God looking at himself, or herself, or Itself. When you think, God thinks. When you speak, God speaks. When you move, God moves. You can say Tao or Brahman the point is you are already liberated. For a long time, it will seem as if you're not realizing this but all change is subtle and exponential in nature.

"Even God cannot have man's mode of knowledge and enjoyment without becoming man"- Woodroffe

This is the nature of an exponential reality. There are infinite effects which we cannot see and cannot know. We can try our best to understand them or predict them but really, there's nothing we really know. These effects are the ones that really make the magic happen. By letting go of a single illusion, you also let go of the Self and fall into a gap, a time dissolving gap called reality.

Not Knowing

The central philosophy of Taoism is an expression termed Wu Wei, which translates to 'do nothing' or 'inaction'. By doing nothing, one has no desires. Man becomes desireless. But the flip side is he shall gain the

world. This type of counter-intuitive reasoning is a central aspect of Taoism.

On the surface of it, it seems like Taoism advocates becoming a couch potato if you wish to experience enlightenment. This impression is a result of viewing the philosophy using our daily constructs or through the lens of Maya. What it really means is that desire brings resistance against natural forces and so is fruitless in results.

In other words, do not fight for what you truly want. Things like desires and material possessions can potentially limit us from reaching our true potential since we become slaves to them. This is why desirelessness is a key aspect of the Tao. It isn't about having little or no possessions or living like a monk. It is about not taking on unnecessary burdens. One cannot explore the world if her world is holding her back, after all.

Wu Wei provides us a framework of dealing with change in this manner. By simply relaxing into acceptance and by viewing everything in terms of its fundamental nature, we adapt better and live better lives. Thus, by accepting the state of desirelessness one can be in accords with the entire universe. If one does wish to act in some way, they would be wise to do so in accordance

with the fundamental laws of nature and follow the path of least resistance or least energy expenditure.

Hopefully, you can see how contrary to linear thought all of this is. The very idea of doing nothing to get what you want makes no sense when viewed in a linear fashion. After all, by doing nothing, you're affecting nothing and if nothing can be affected, how can the thing further down the line move.

Linear thought is all about activity and grabbing things. Non-linear thinking requires you to allow things to come to you. You never know the true extent of the consequences of actions (or inaction), the mind cannot know any future; however hard it tries to grasp it. Sure, you might be able to utilize the power of the law of attraction, but you can never know the pathway the present moment takes to materialize your dreams.

Children are great at manifesting for the simple reason of always being aware and in flow. This is pretty much how our childhood years fly past. But then we begin to learn one linear habit after another and develop all sorts of mental unease. Anxiety and depression are at their highest levels worldwide, and by understanding the connection between linear thought and the unawareness of non-linear thought, we can see how these disorders develop.

The keys to resolving the obstacles of the future lie in the wisdom of the past. In many ways, this shows that no matter how far we move in terms of technology or culture; ultimately, the universe is momentary and fluid.

CHAPTER 7

The Dream of Waking Life

We've explored the nature of reality quite a bit, but there are still some holes in our knowledge. You see, exploring something outside of ourselves is all well and good, but of what use is this if we don't understand the underlying illusion we're trapped in? So far, we've skirted by this topic by saying that illusions ought to be ignored, but that's a lot like saying you need to give up smoking.

How exactly do you carry out this task? Thankfully, doing this is a lot easier than giving up smoking. The combination of your knowledge and awareness of the characteristics of your waking life will put you in a good position to call the illusory world's bluff.

Brahman

I've mentioned the existence of the concept of Brahman as explained in Vedanta philosophy previously in this book. Vedanta has two branches within it, one nondual called Advaita and the other dual called Dvaita. Advaita Vedanta states that Brahman is our very nature itself. We carry an incomplete piece of it with us wherever we go, much like every other living creature does.

I won't be touching on Dvaita Vedanta here since its propositions are not of any particular use to us and remain academic. Following the reasoning of Advaita, we arrive at the existence of a soul within us, called Atman, which is our true self and is a piece of Brahman. Whether you consider Atman as a piece of the overall picture that is Brahman, or just a reflection of it is beside the point.

The key thing to learn here is you carry a piece of divinity within you, and that's why enlightenment is about realizing or freeing yourself from binds, as Buddha stated, instead of learning some new philosophy. The qualities you desire are already within you. You simply need to clear the clouds that obscure it.

Maya

If Brahman is the sunshine in our existence, then Maya is the cloud cover that obscures it. The difficult thing about Maya to grasp is that it begins at some point after our physical birth; we just don't know when it exactly began. Maya is imposed upon us through our environment and the superego.

The ego can be viewed as a piece of Maya and can be thought of as its best friend. Indeed, the ego is fueled by Maya and the illusory world. Maya causes us to misinterpret the reality of our existence and to attach huge importance to our physical body. After all, the body and its senses are how we experience both Maya. We begin to fear harm to our body, fear death, and try to control the illusion.

How can someone grasp and control something that isn't there? This is quite impossible. Hence, a cycle of frustration begins and we enter a vicious circle where we grasp the unreal and become frustrated with our attempts to control something that isn't even there.

Ignorance, pain, hatred, and so on come spewing forth and all of this is fertile territory for the ego to sink its roots. In short, we literally create our own hell. Maya

is constantly moving, like a motion picture we see on a screen. Brahman can be thought of as the background, the screen itself. You can't experience Maya (movie) without at the same time experiencing Brahman (screen).

Therefore, Brahman is not a God or something to be worshipped. It is merely a reality that needs to be realized and remembered through awareness and deep contemplation. While watching a movie, you tend to forget about the screen. Liberation is seeing the screen and movie playing together. On the surface of it, this doesn't square with the notion of a bigger intelligence existing beyond us that guides us through life. Well, the answer to this question lies in examining the purpose of religion.

True religion is all about pointing a person towards reality. The stuff about worshipping this God and not that one, about eating this food and not that food, is a result of the writers of these tenets becoming consumed by Maya, or whatever word that religion uses to describe it. Reality is not something that can be described and grasped by words, as we saw in the previous chapter.

Hence the major problem that religion has is to translate something that cannot be translated. It does this by using familiar language and hence the notion of God appears. The prospect of an all-knowing state of being is

tough to understand. Logically, we can reason that some-thing like Brahman has to exist since being (our physical form) cannot come into existence from nonbeing. To deny this logic is to deny the existence of our own being which doesn't make sense.

Philosophical tracts, which lend themselves better to abstract topics, describe Brahman as pure consciousness. Thus, Brahman is real, but it is not a being. Rather it is a state which is only experienced and whether or not it has a physical form is unknown. Brahman is pure joy and is all knowing. It is the same knowing that knows your experience. When you touch a physical object who is it that knows you are touching? And it's definitely not the ego.

Brahman implies freedom from all of this. There is no reason to know anything, no reason to feel joy or sadness, and no compulsion. In this freedom lies the essence of all life; Bliss. Western philosophy often misinterprets this negatively which leads to the path of 'nothing matters, so why bother' type of thinking. However, this is a false construct since it goes squarely against Brahman's impli-cation of the purification of the soul.

Moksha, which I touched upon in the first chapter, is the way to the realization of reality. Moksha implies com-

plete freedom from Maya. A death that lets go of an individual completely, no more need to cling onto THIS life. This freedom is realized not through language or thought but through intuition.

Intuition is the language that Brahman and consciousness speak in. As you can imagine, it is difficult to put the feeling of intuition into words and this is precisely why you won't find too many works dealing with the ins and outs of Brahman. It is far more helpful to us, as unconscious beings, to understand what it 'isn't' rather than what it 'is'.

'Not' is what Maya and all of its illusions are. The concept of reincarnation can be understood as a soul's journey through Maya, starting with the lowest level, where the prospect of even recognizing the existence of it is not possible. Each physical life can be viewed as the progressive purification of the soul.

This is why some people undergo hell on Earth, seemingly, because of the overall journey that their soul needs to take in order to attain Moksha. Of course, one is free to reject the lessons that life provides us with and regress in our ability to attain salvation. You will recognize the traditional religious concepts of hell and heaven in this philosophy. The notion of repenting for your sins is simply twisted interpretations of this philosophy.

If Maya doesn't matter and if reality needs to only be felt, then how does one live their life? Well, awareness is a huge step. Recognizing the unreality of Maya and how it seeks to consume you through constructs which don't matter all that much is what brings awareness. There will be a degree up to which you can disregard Maya and this is the degree to which you are enlightened. Meditation and turning inward help with the process greatly. The mere act of moving closer to the nature of reality by maintaining a curious child-like view and a present mind is the catalyst by which you will recognize the illusory nature of this world. Often during deep meditation, you will be plunged into a pure experience of oneself before snapping out of it.

These glimpses of Brahman are more than enough to bring you closer to reality. Reality is not a goal, but it is what is already there. Aiming for something that you already have is a bit nonsensical. Hence, relaxing and resting into yourself, like taking a seat in your being, are the keys to clearing the clouds of Maya.

Waking Up to Life

What does it mean to wake up? Exploring the nature of waking up is important because there is the danger of you

turning this into a goal of sorts and thereby introducing duality into your life. A lot of spiritual 'gurus' indulge in this sort of thinking by drawing an unconscious line between themselves and others.

Even worse, some people become obsessed with discovering reality and begin to neglect their current existence and mistreat themselves or those around them. Remember that the ego works by placing yourself in both a superior and inferior position. True spiritual awakening is anti-climactic by nature. Your existence doesn't change all that much and you simply become more of yourself.

You will not begin to fly in the air or hypnotize ropes into forming ladders, as is often depicted in orientalist books. As I mentioned before, how would anything change if you uncover something that is already there? The point of liberation is not the goal but the current path you are on. This is why discharging duties as intended along the way and listening to the voice of reality, via your emotion, is extremely important.

The path itself is not a bed of roses. This doesn't mean it will be fully unpleasant, but don't expect it to be only full of joy. Spiritual awakening is you rising from a deep sleep so you can expect some grogginess and a feeling of being an uncoordinated mess that takes some time to get used to.

This is often the case when people snap out of Maya via a sudden insight, much like how we sometimes wake up in the middle of the night and are fully conscious. We know we need to go back to sleep and are aware that we've woken up, but it feels like half our brain is missing. In such moments you can literally feel the rest of your brain trying to catch up and this results in a few moments of confusion and disorientation.

While the new reality, or true reality, takes some getting used to, you will realize that you are deeply moved by the things around you. You will begin to view everything as it really is. The people around you are as connected to you as your fingers are to your body. Causing them harm is the same as chopping a part of you away and brings the same level of pain.

If you happen to be emotionally dead to other people and their concerns don't resonate with you in any way, you are quite far from a spiritual awakening. If you are moved by their concerns, do whatever you can to alleviate the situation. You will realize that while you can help with as much sincerity as possible, ultimately it is they who need to free themselves.

Learning about the nature of reality doesn't stop once you're awake spiritually. If anything, the degree

with which you will begin to explore your existence will increase dramatically and you will find that your environment gives you opportunities to increase the level of your awareness.

The Comfort of Ignorance

Many of us choose to spend our lives asleep. We might be walking around with our eyes open and interacting with the world, but this is merely interaction with Maya and only strengthens the illusion that enslaves us. Spirituality is a tool to help us wake up, an alarm clock if you will.

Waking up is usually a painful experience. Most of us would rather hit the snooze button and continue to enjoy the warmth of our bed. However, do this long enough and it's easy to see how harmful this can be. Remaining spiritually ignorant works in the same way. Unfortunately, there is no blaring alarm to make us get up. Instead, what happens is a painful upheaval in our lives.

This upheaval could be something that happens to us, or to someone close to us. Either way, the longer you ignore the call of spirituality, the greater the degree of life will just be happening to you, just as a nonlucid dream 'happens' to the dreamer. Life will become, in a sense pre-ordained, your purpose will be chosen by the cur-

rent. Ignoring the spiritual aspect of nature is simply not going to work in your favor, unless you happen to be a masochist and enjoy causing emotional pain for yourself and those around you.

Some of us shut ourselves away and remain in our comfort zone because we fear the risks may be too great. The potential for pain is high, and we instinctively avoid living fully. Our ego convinces us that true bliss is living without pain. What we fail to recognize is that pain is simply the other side of the coin that also contains happiness and fulfillment. Without one, you can't have the other.

Therefore, sleeping in your bed is only going to make you lazy and sick of everything. Human beings were born into this world to push boundaries. Stifling yourself is going against your natural instincts. Yes, there is the prospect of pain. However, there is also an equal prospect of great rewards.

Living wide awake can be painful but is ultimately the most rewarding method of living since the rewards come from truth, instead of Maya. When you are awake, there is no sense of identity. You know what your name is and what you do for a living and so on, but you don't attach overbearing significance to it. You realize that you are as fluid and ever-changing as the world is and that trying to somehow contain or control this truth is pointless.

Waking up spiritually allows you to increase the amount of love in your life, and when you see yourself as part of a whole, you recognize the fallacy of the lone wolf thought process. The idea that you need to do everything yourself and that this is a sign of strength is a mostly masculine construct that has its place. There is certainly nothing wrong with it.

However, ultimate reality always needs you to develop connections with those around you in order to progress. Even those who think of themselves as lone wolves end up realizing that their progress could not have happened without the assistance of the people around them. Life always provides you with the chance to grow and stretch. Grab it with both hands, even if the immediate outcome seems painful.

Living in truth is perhaps the best way to free yourself. After all, what is freer than a being which is constantly in motion and is constantly expanding? Paradoxically, this freedom is precisely what scares us because it implies infinite possibilities and an exponential reality. We simply cannot project in a linear fashion all the possible outcomes that will occur from us choosing to wake up.

This is why the act of surrender to a higher power, be it God or the universe or whatever construct you choose,

is so powerful. By surrendering, you remove the responsibility of the result from yourself. You are only in control of your actions and not the result.

Living fully awake is the only way to live, really. It is challenging and scary, but it sure is worth it. Understand the wisdom in this by using the principles of nonduality and the interconnectedness of everything.

Lucid Living

What does it mean to live lucidly? Lucidity implies clarity or something that is bright. Lucid dreaming is the process of waking up when you're dreaming and realizing that what you're experiencing is not real. All of us experience dreams and nightmares when we sleep. While the reason for this is not known scientifically, it has been postulated that dreams are a byproduct of the brain assimilating new information.

We usually take part in our dreams unconsciously, believing that what we're experiencing is reality and accepting the resultant emotions as real. Nightmares can be truly torturous to go through and often shock us to the extent that they wake us from a deep sleep. Lucid dreaming is the process of waking up in the dream and recognizing the dream world for what it truly is.

People who dream lucidly often report a feeling of calmness that descends upon them once they realize that their current experience is not real and is a mental hallucination. This allows them to observe what is going on with greater clarity and draw conclusions from it. Dreams can lead to a more fulfilling life because they sometimes contain answers to real-life problems.

Lucid living is simply extending the dream concept to reality. To live lucidly is to recognize the reality in which you live. A lot of us are simply living within Maya and are reacting to its provocations, much like we would inside a dream. To live lucidly is to question your state of consciousness and awareness constantly and to test whether your assumptions of the current situation are valid.

Living in this manner is like a breath of fresh air. As we allow truth to come to us, we find ourselves energized and motivated to really live life as it is meant to be. This is simply you recognizing the need to follow your purpose and to take steps towards it. Whether you achieve it or not is beside the point. Lucidity provides you with the power of great influence over your life.

You will also begin to recognize the folly of those around you who constantly react to Maya and burden themselves with all sorts of constructs. Help them as

much as you can, but not to the extent of harming yourself. You will see that they are receiving lessons of their own to learn, and this will help them liberate themselves when their time comes, whether in this life or the next.

Lucid living will be disorienting at first since you will question the reality of everything around you, and considering whether something as solid as a wall is real or not can be disconcerting. This isn't some Nirvana for you to aim at, and treating it in this manner will only cause you to place undue importance on things that are not real.

To live lucidly is to become fully aware of your behavior and to recognize how Maya programs you to react unconsciously. You will realize that nothing in this world can possibly harm you since it is all unimportant. The truth of love and abundance will flow to you and will enable you to live the most prosperous and comfortable life imaginable.

This seems paradoxical to a lot of people. Ideas such as understanding nonduality through duality, of attaining freedom by surrendering, and of becoming free through discipline reflect the deep divide between Maya and the truth. Take the time to really understand the truth of your existence and listen to your intuition. Allow them to guide you to your ultimate purpose.

Achieving your purpose is not an easy task. This does not mean it is an unpleasant one. While living lucidly, you will be deeply engaged and inspired in achieving what truly matters to you and obstacles will simply appear to be speed bumps. You will recognize your obstacles to be the learning experiences that they truly are. Without learning, there can be no expansion, and this is what obstacles provide you with.

It seems funny to say this, but you will wish for obstacles to present themselves since you cannot grow without them. After all, what is the fun in driving along an empty, characterless, straight road? You need some curves and scenery to spice things up!

The truly wise people in our world learn from not just their own experiences but from those of others as well. Learn from the mistakes and the successes of those before you. They have already invented the wheel and there is no need for you to reinvent it. Your task is to improve it and enable the universe to expand exponentially. At the end of the day, the purpose of every living being boils down to this fact.

The best way to induce lucid living in your life is to maintain the Buddhist principles of the middle path. Avoid extreme situations in anything, even in your belief

about true reality. What I mean to say is, don't take my word for what reality really is, go discover it yourself. Get curious about it and develop your own conclusions. To question and discover is the most scientific thing to do. You will find during your discovery that the primary principles of academia, science, and spirituality concur with one another.

Take for example the theory of exponentiality. I propose this is a universal truth because of the way natural phenomena occur. Consider the concept of patient zero in studies regarding epidemics. The idea that one person or thing can spread disease shows that it spreads exponentially, not linearly.

Consider further the subject of neuroscience. When you seek to replace an old neural network with a new one by repetition, it is not just the old network that gets deactivated. The networks that support the old, incorrect network stop firing as well in the context which triggers the false network. This does not happen consciously but automatically. This is evidence of exponentiality within our brains.

Consider the way a space shuttle is launched into space. Once it leaves Earth, the shuttle does not need any more thrust because if thrust (that is, acceleration) was

constantly applied, the shuttle would simply disintegrate thanks to the high speed it would attain. When acceleration is constant, velocity increases exponentially. This is a fundamental law in physics. When working on big tasks, you need to keep hammering away constantly until you achieve a breakthrough (critical mass) and then progress comes in droves. This is simply exponentiality at work.

I could go on and on. My point is that by observing phenomena across different fields, often unconnected; you will begin to see patterns that inform you of the truth of existence. The Buddha himself prescribed an attitude of curiosity when seeking truth via meditation. He taught his followers not to believe a word he said and to seek truth themselves. Religion has forgotten this basic fact and has tragically made peasants of men.

I say tragically because this act has raised a wall between us and truth and has created an artificial divide between spirituality and science. The goals of both endeavors are the same: to explain the truth. The methods are exactly the same. Experimentation and discovery allied with honesty. This is what lucid living is all about.

So wake up from your slumber and open your eyes to the beauty all around you!

Conclusion

The dream state we live our lives in convinces us that misfortune, disease and depression are the only states of being. Maya equally convinces some of us that joy, love, compassion, and goodness are the only states of being. My hope throughout this book has been to show you that neither of these extreme views is true. Liberation is ultimately about recognizing nonduality through dual constructs.

When viewed in this manner, you will begin to see Maya the way the Vedas have seen it, as a creative device. It is not your enemy but is actually an incomplete piece of the whole. It is your perception that paints it as either your friend or your enemy. Change your perception and you will change your world.

I don't mean to say that the universe is unkind or that Biblical exhortations are the absolute truth. No, this is a misinterpretation. The universe or Brahman is an

enabler that helps us reach what we desire. If we desire to bury ourselves deeply in Maya, this is what happens. It will provide us with lessons about the importance of getting back to ourselves, but ultimately these lessons get buried under the misery that Maya provides. In other words, Man becomes the device for illusions to express themselves.

If we wish to seek the truth, the universe enables this. We begin to view Maya as just a tool and see it for what it is. Liberation is therefore entirely down to your intention. Set your intention in accordance with your purpose and you will achieve the results you desire. Can it be that some people's desire or purpose is to live in Maya? Well, it is possible. After all, no one knows what the bigger plan is. Perhaps by burying themselves in Maya in this life, the soul seeks to learn a lesson that will aid its progress to Moksha in the next.

Much like how some people were perfectly content to live inside the Matrix, in the movie of the same name, because they just weren't ready to accept true reality, some of us are engineered in this manner. This is precisely why it is important to let your heart speak to you and to give it space. Recognize that everything has a reason to exist, even if it is the most unspeakable evil.

Good and bad or any forms of duality are just representations of the same coin, and one cannot exist without the other. The biggest cause of misery and suffering in your life is your inability to recognize the truth about your existence. The various chapters in this book have each spoken about a different facet of reality and you now can take the time to really understand what was said.

Cutting Bonds

The process of liberation is not easy to carry out. Your ego and superego will convince you that the bonds you sever are the ones tethering you to life. A practical example of this is letting go of people in your life who constantly bring you down. Sadly, for most of us, these people happen to be family members.

Does this mean you should cut all contact? Well, that is perhaps taking too drastic a step. Committing to an extreme solution should never be your first choice, so take the time to measure your response appropriately. Minimize contact as much as possible. If this is not realistic, then seek to change your environment as much as possible. In other words, remove yourself from the situation instead of seeking to remove others from your life.

Some steps you take will seem drastic and you will observe a reaction from your current peer group. If this

reaction is negative, simply smile and go about your business. This is easier said than done of course. We will experience pain when our friends and family begin to reject us as we awaken spiritually. Experiencing pain is a part of life and you should not banish it or suppress it in a quest to feel good.

The feel good movement has sprung from a misunderstanding about the law of attraction. Due to this, most people begin to think that since truth is all about love and nurturing, negativity is somehow false and is a part of Maya. This is a complete distortion of reality. Remember, that reality is just an enabler whose full aims are not known. We have all the tools in front of us. We just need to use them.

Instead of aiming to feel good, aim to feel better. If you've suffered the loss of a loved one, only a lunatic would prescribe that you need to reject the sadness that accompanies you. True liberation is about accepting the pain and giving it space without letting it take over your entire life. Do not turn it into something greater than what it is.

Pain is something most people do not deal well with and often end up using it to define themselves. Perversely, some people use negativity to spur them on to greater

heights. A slight, an admonishment, an insult, and so on are used to achieve seemingly great things. This is an imbalanced state of being, and eventually, the universe rectifies the imbalance by removing the consequences of it. Thus, if you achieved success thanks to overly negative thoughts, success vanishes.

The Ego

Detachment from the ego is the big step you need to take in order to free yourself. However, the method of doing this can get a bit complicated. This is because the ego can trick you into supporting it if your understanding of reality is flawed. This is why it is important to take the time to understand reality before trying to let go of the ego.

"Let go" is the operative phrase here. Do not assume a martial stance against it since this will merely put you in a position where you will derive your identity from such a position. Seeing the world as being a struggle between you and your ego is to invite failure.

Keep in mind that the ego and its constructs wish to keep the world as static as possible. Reality is fluid and exponential. Our minds cannot comprehend this using language since language is a linear construct we have developed to explain Maya. True reality exists beyond

this and it is inexplicable using worldly mechanisms. You will need to feel your way forward and this will seem disorienting at first.

Above all else, always return to the awareness of reality if you feel directionless. Embrace your emotions fully, even negative ones, and give them space to bloom while remaining as equanimous as possible. The path to liberation lies in the middle. Embrace it, and you will achieve everything you want.

I wish you the best of luck in your journey and all the happiness in the world!

References

3 steps to 'spiritual awakening' by raising your brain waves to gamma! (2019). Retrieved 22 August 2019, from https://medium.com/@yelizruzgar/3-steps-to-spiritual-awakening-by-raising-your-brain-waves-to-gamma-11f93d66146a

Brain waves, yoga, and meditation. (2019). Retrieved 22 August 2019, from http://www.yogatoeaseanxiety.com/blog/brain-waves-yoga-and-meditation

Boghani, P. (2017). *How poverty can follow children into adulthood*. Retrieved 27 August 2019, from https://www.pbs.org/wgbh/frontline/article/how-poverty-can-follow-children-into-adulthood/

Cherry, K. (2019). *Achieve the 'flow' mindset to get the job done*. Retrieved 27 August 2019, from https://www.verywellmind.com/what-is-flow-2794768

Clear, J. (2019). *The 3 r's of habit change: How to start new habits that actually stick.* Retrieved 22 August 2019, from https://jamesclear.com/three-steps-habit-change

Izsak, M. (2006). *"The Matrix" review: An in-depth analysis of the groundbreaking sci-fi film.* Retrieved 27 August 2019, from http://www.lyratek.com/matrix01.htm

Jackson, A. (2019). *CUBAN: Don't go to school for finance - liberal arts is the future.* Retrieved 22 August 2019, from https://www.businessinsider.in/CUBAN-Dont-go-to-school-for-finance-liberal-arts-is-the-future/articleshow/57214655.cms

Maltz, M. (2015). *Psycho-Cybernetics.* New York: Perigee, an imprint of Penguin Random House LLC.

Mchardy, J. (2009*). The universal laws that create your future.* Retrieved 27 August 2019, from https://www.streetdirectory.com/travel_guide/155284/motivation/the_universal_laws_that_create_your_future.html

Moore, C. (2019). *What is eudaimonia? Aristotle and eudaimonic well-being.* Retrieved 22 August 2019, from https://positivepsychology.com/eudaimonia/

Nadler, S. (2016). *Baruch Spinoza (Stanford Encyclopedia of Philosophy)*. Retrieved 22 August 2019, from https://plato.stanford.edu/entries/spinoza/

Niels Bohr - Important scientists - The physics of the universe. (2019). Retrieved 22 August 2019, from https://www.physicsoftheuniverse.com/scientists_bohr.html

Palermo, E. (2017). *Niels Bohr: biography & atomic theory*. Retrieved 27 August 2019, from https://www.livescience.com/32016-niels-bohr-atomic-theory.html

Popova, M. (2019). Alan Watts on the antidote to the loneliness of the divided mind, our integration with the universe, and how we wrest meaning from reality. Retrieved 22 August 2019, from https://www.brainpickings.org/2016/11/01/alan-watts-wisdom-of-insecurity-3/

Redd, N. (2019). *Einstein's theory of general relativity*. Retrieved 22 August 2019, from https://www.space.com/17661-theory-general-relativity.html

The science of spirituality: A psychologist and a neuroscientist explain being 'in the flow'. (2019). Retrieved 22 August 2019, from https://www.forbes.com/sites/alicegwalton/2017/08/22/the-science-of-spirituality-a-psychologist-and-a-neuroscientist-explain-being-in-the-flow/#39828a7b4e0b

Thum, M. (2008). *Clock time vs. Psychological time.* Retrieved 27 August 2019, from https://www.myrkothum. com/the-difference-of-clock-time-and-psychological-time/

Waking up spiritually. (2019). Retrieved 22 August 2019, from https://www.hazelden.org/web/public/apr-13wakingupspiritually.page

What is oneness? (2019). Retrieved 22 August 2019, from https://www.healyourlife.com/what-is-oneness

What is stoicism? A simple definition & 10 stoic core principles. (2019). Retrieved 27 August 2019, from https://www.njlifehacks.com/what-is-stoicism-over-view-definition-10-stoic-principles/

A Short message
from the Author

Hey, have you enjoyed A Life of Liberation? I'd love to hear your thoughts!

Many readers do not know how hard reviews are to come by, and how much they help an author.

I would be incredibly grateful if you could take just 60 seconds to write a brief review on Amazon, even if it's just a few sentences!

>> Scan the QR Code above to leave a quick review <<

Thank you for taking the time to share your thoughts!

Your review will genuinely make a difference for me and help gain exposure for my work